AM I.....A PEOPLE PLEASER?

Codependency and the Childhood Trauma that Creates Relationship Addicts

BY

ELENA MIRO

Copyright Info

© Copyright Elena Miro 2023 - All rights reserved.

The content contained within this book may not be reproduced, duplicated, or transmitted without direct written permission from the author or the publisher except for the use of brief quotations in a book review.

Under no circumstances will any blame or legal responsibility be held against the publisher, or author, for any damages, reparation, or monetary loss due to the information contained within this book. Either directly or indirectly. You are responsible for your own choices, actions, and results.

Legal Notice:

This book is copyright protected. This book is only for personal use. You cannot amend, distribute, sell, use, quote or paraphrase any part, or the content within this book, without the consent of the author or publisher except for the use of brief quotations in a book review.

Disclaimer notice:

Please note the information contained within this book is for educational and entertainment purposes only. All effort has been executed to present accurate, up to date, and reliable, complete information. No warranties of any kind are declared or implied. Readers acknowledge that the author is not engaging in the rendering of legal, financial, medical, or professional advice. The content within this book has been derived from various sources. Please consult a licensed professional before attempting any techniques outlined in this book.

By reading this book, the reader agrees that under no circumstances is the author responsible for any losses, direct or indirect, which are incurred as a result of the use of the information contained within this book, including, but not limited to,—errors, omissions, or inaccuracies.

Table of Contents

Chapter 1: *The House that Built You and Your Attachment Style* 10

Chapter 2: *Childhood Trauma and Human Psychosocial Development* 37

Chapter 3: *The Psychology of Codependency* 54

Chapter 4: *The Signs of Relationship Addiction* 68

Chapter 5: *Your Restless Inner Child* 84

Chapter 6: *Gifts from the Shadows* 97

Chapter 7: *From Denial to Acceptance* 113

Chapter 8: *So You're Codependent—What Now?* 124

Chapter 9: *The Road to a Solution – First Steps* 137

References Cited 141

A Word from the Author

For much of my life, I've felt less than whole. I worked hard to try to please the people I loved, but I still didn't feel good about myself. My self-esteem was very low. I felt like I was always on the edge, waiting for one tiny bit of criticism to push me off. What's more, I found that because I didn't value myself, I was neglecting my needs. I always put myself last. At the time, I thought I was just being a good daughter, sister, girlfriend, wife, and so on. I thought I needed to sacrifice myself so others could be happy. It was so ingrained in my personality that I didn't even think of it as a sacrifice; I just thought of it as the standard behavior of someone who loves the people around them. But no matter what I did, I didn't feel like I was a good person. I couldn't understand what else I needed to do. I never thought my problem could be the result of patterns of behavior that began in my childhood. I didn't recognize that it could be the product of childhood trauma. Sure, my family had its share of problems, but nobody physically beat me. I could never have imagined that there are other types of abuse so subtle that you wouldn't even recognize them. I always thought my childhood was okay and sometimes even good. But when I really began delving into my patterns of behavior, I started to see that not everything was as good as I had initially thought. In fact, I came to understand just how dysfunctional my family dynamic had been. Working on my personal growth and experiencing dramatic changes in my life prompted me to pursue a degree in psychology. Now, I want to help other people experience those beneficial changes too.

If any of this resonates with you, you might have the same type of problem that I discovered I have. It's called codependency, and it's an insidious pattern that you develop in childhood and carry into adulthood. It sets you up for failure and can make you a target for abusers. In fact, it's common for codependents to seek out abusers in their life because they recognize them in one way or another. As an adult, you don't often see this pattern in your life. You also don't usually think too much about your childhood and how it might be affecting your life today. But some powerful issues can develop in childhood which could cause even bigger problems as an adult. Do you notice any of the following patterns in your own life today:

- Low self-esteem
- A history of toxic adult relationships
- A strong fear of loneliness
- Problems with addiction (alcohol, drugs, or food)
- A sense of worthlessness
- A strong need to please the people you love so they won't leave you
- A feeling of emptiness that you can't seem to resolve
- Fear of abandonment
- Problems making decisions
- Poor boundaries

- Caretaking behaviors
- Trouble identifying your thoughts, needs, feelings, or desires

If you identify most of these symptoms in yourself, then you might be codependent too. Please note that you are not alone—approximately 50% of the population is codependent. In fact, in one study of over 500 people, 64% of participants showed high levels of codependency. Some estimates suggest that it's possible that more than 90% of the US population exhibits at least some codependent behaviors. This is a very common problem, and it can have a dramatic effect on your quality of life.

I know because it definitely affected my life. I spent a good deal of time studying this problem, both professionally as a psychotherapist and personally as a codependent. I have been through two painful divorces, and I've experienced at least two more codependent relationships. I know how it feels to feel like you desperately need the other people in your life. I also know how it feels to think your childhood was normal until you dig a little deeper and find out that there really were problems. We only have our experience to work from, and until you learn there are other ways of living, it's quite common to idealize the version of childhood that you had. But the kind of childhood that causes codependency can make you terrified of being abandoned. You may become willing to do almost anything someone you love demands so they won't leave you. You feel like you will literally die if they do, but I can also tell you, you won't. There is a way out of this madness. There is a way to live the life of your dreams, have inner freedom, and love without strings of fear attached because you know you're enough by yourself. It took me a long time to find that way out, but I very much want to share what I have learned with you. This book is all about giving you the answers you might not know you're seeking but desperately need. It's about helping you discover the truth so you can move toward a real solution.

That's what I want to share with you in this book; all the ways you can become a people pleaser. I will show you just how your family story and behavioral patterns contributed to your codependency. I will help you understand how your parents shaped your understanding of yourself and your role in life and how the beliefs from your childhood shaped you into the adult you have become. I'll discuss how your psychosocial development was disrupted as a result of the trauma (obvious or not) you endured as a child. I'll examine in-depth the psychology of codependency, the symptoms that indicate you might have this problem, how it would affect your inner child, and how it shapes your view of your shadow self. I'll also help you understand how to move from denial of your problem to acceptance and what you can do once you've reached that important stage. I'll help you toward finding a solution so you can begin healing the trauma. Then, in my second book on this subject—*Healing Codependency: How to Resolve Your Childhood Trauma so You Can Start Living Your Best Life*—I'll take you step-by-step through the healing journey.

These books are filled with helpful exercises for you to use to understand yourself better and find solutions tailored to your situation. I'll talk about the most current research on the subject, what experts have learned through the years about the delicate human psyche, and the many ways it can be harmed. I'll help you recognize what may be subtle clues in your situation that indicate you are codependent. I'll stand beside you as you face that which contributed to the problem in your childhood. I didn't want to believe anything bad about my own mother, but I had to face the painful reality that she was abusive in ways I couldn't see at first.

I'll help you do that too. It's not easy. It takes courage. In fact, it may be the most courageous thing you ever do in your lifetime. It's painful and frightening to look closely into the house that built you, but that's where you must start to truly understand why you are the way you are. Don't worry—I'll be right there with you, and we'll take this journey together. Let's begin by examining your early life story and how that may have shaped your attachment style.

Don't be afraid…together we are strong! Together, we can heal!

Chapter 1

The House that Built You and Your Attachment Style

We see the world through the lens of our experiences. What happens to us from the moment we are born shapes our psyche and helps to build us into who we will become. For six years, I was in psychotherapy. For many more years, I studied psychology, and I have worked with numerous clients as a psychotherapist. During that time, I was really searching for myself. I was examining the minute details of my own story, my own trauma, and every little thing that made me into the person I am now. It's a journey we all eventually take. It's a struggle to understand why we are the way we are. But sometimes, you need more information to learn just how you came to be and how even the earliest years of your childhood could have had a significant impact on your self-identity. It all begins with how you learn to view the world. That forms the basis for your attachment style and a blueprint for your psychosocial development.

The Early Years and Your Attachment Style

I was not born as a result of love. My mother made this clear to me very early in my life. She never loved my biological father; she loved another man whom she had met years before. He broke her heart, and she never believed she would love again. She told my father that she didn't love him, but he so deeply loved her that he assured her, "My love will be more than enough for the two of us." It might have been enough for the two of them, but it wasn't enough for me. As I said, I was not a baby born of love, and as a result, I was not given the kind of love that would help me form a healthy attachment style. Even as a child, I could sense that somehow, I was not enough. I was also a disappointment to my father, who wanted a boy. Just one more disappointment that even infants can sense.

How do infants sense their parents' emotions? They see in the faces of their parents and feel it in their touch. These visual and physical sensations are how infants experience the world, and that's how they will form their view of what the world is like. Do their parents mirror love with kind, happy, satisfied eyes, or do they display disappointment with apathy or irritation? Children also feel it in touch and embrace, or lack thereof, that conveys those kinds of messages. Is it warm and tender, or cold and clinical? They understand it when they cry and no one comes to help them. This is how they get their initial impression of the world. A preverbal infant has no way of letting someone know they need something other than by crying. When those cries are not answered, they learn that sometimes, their needs may not be met. It teaches them that the world can be an uncaring place.

A man named John Bowlby—a British psychoanalyst—was the first person to attempt to understand the concept of attachment. He described the behaviors of infants who were separated from primary caregivers and noted that some infants went to extreme lengths to prevent separation from their parents and reestablish a secure proximity. Many researchers at the time had attributed the distress as the result of immature defense mechanisms, but Bowlby argued that it was an adaptive response shaped by evolutionary forces, given that similar behaviors are often seen in other mammalian species. Like humans, they are dependent upon the adults to care for and protect them until they are developed enough to do so for themselves. Bowlby argued that those with a more secure attachment would be more likely to survive to reproductive age, which explains how natural selection likely shaped the attachment behavioral system.

Attachment Styles Defined

While Bowlby recognized the attachment dynamics, it was his colleague, Mary Ainsworth, who did the experiments that allowed her to identify individual differences in attachment styles. She separated 12-month-old infants from their parents, and then observed their reactions when they were reunited. She found that there were three basic styles:

❖ Secure Attachment Style

The children with this attachment style exhibited what Bowlby called **normative behavior**. They were upset when separated from their parents, but when the parent returned, they sought them out and were easily comforted by them. About 60% of the children who participated in the experiments were identified as having a secure attachment style.

❖ Anxious-Resistant Attachment Style

Some, about 20% or fewer, of the children who participated in the experiments were found to have what came to be called an **anxious-resistant** attachment style. These children were ill-at-ease in the strange setting of the laboratory, but when they were separated from their parents, they became extremely distressed. Once reunited with their parents, it was still difficult to soothe them, and they exhibited conflicting behaviors that indicated that, although they wanted to be comforted, they also wanted to punish their parents for leaving.

❖ Avoidant Attachment Style

Another 20% of children exhibited an **avoidant** attachment style. These children did not appear very distressed when separated from their parents. When they were reunited, they actively *avoided* seeking contact with the parent, in contrast with the previous attachment styles we discussed.

❖ Disorganized/Disoriented Attachment Style:

Since those early experiments by Ainsworth, other researchers identified another attachment style in 1986. This is the **disorganized/disoriented** or **fearful-avoidant** attachment style. Like the other insecure attachment styles, it stems from childhood trauma or neglect. Individuals with this attachment style feel like they don't deserve love or closeness. They never learned to self-soothe as children, and as a result, they feel confused and unsettled in relationships as they experience emotional extremes. These would be the children in Ainsworth's study who exhibited a mixture of behaviors associated with both anxious-resistant and avoidant attachment styles.

Perhaps the most important finding from Ainsworth's and Main and Solomon's research was that the individual differences in attachment style correlated with interactions between the infant and their parents during the first year of life at home. Many people had presumed that children that young were not affected by their environment and interactions because they couldn't remember it. Ainsworth's research showed that, in fact, even an infant is taking in their experiences and forming beliefs about the world. The children who were more secure in their attachment styles had parents who were responsive to their needs, whereas the children who exhibited the other two styles had parents who were insensitive to their needs. They may have been inconsistent in their responses, or they may have outright rejected their responsibilities in providing for the infant.

My experience during the first two years of my life was one of rejection and insensitivity. My own mother stopped breastfeeding me at two weeks of age. She had no reason for doing so, but later said it was because my father was unsupportive of her needs. At six months old, my mother was already pregnant with my brother, around that time when her mother died. She was distracted from caring for her infant daughter, to say the least. Her attention was on her mother's death and the child growing inside her. My brother was born a heavy child, and during childbirth, both my mother's and brother's lives were at risk. In fact, the doctor told my father that he had to choose which of them they should save. Fortunately, an experienced midwife saved them both, but it became increasingly apparent that my brother's life was considered more valuable than mine.

Of course, mothers may have a special relationship with their sons and a more complicated one with their daughters, but my mother placed some big demands on me at a very young age. When I was just one year and two months old, she focused on my brother's needs, and my needs fell to a distant second place. I was clearly not her priority, and even a child of such a young age can sense that in a primary caregiver. My mother continuously reinforced that message as I grew older. While my brother and I grew up close and spent lots of time together until our lives took us in different directions, I always felt the weight of my mother's preference for my brother. At a very young age, I was already feeling like I wasn't good enough. I was more of an attendant and less of a beloved child, and this all occurred during the first two years of my life. I can say it definitely affected my attachment style.

Attachment Style Manifesting in Adulthood

The attachment style patterns you develop in your first years tend to persist into adulthood. How you view the world—as a relatively safe place where your needs will be met most of the time, or as a dangerous place where your needs might not be met—greatly affects the behavior patterns you develop as you grow into adulthood. Likewise, these patterns affect the types and nature of the close relationships you form with others. Here are the types of behaviors seen with the different styles.

Secure Attachment Style

Infants with a secure attachment style tend to grow into well-adjusted, resilient children who are well-liked and get along with their peers. As adults, they are more satisfied in their relationships, which are characterized by greater longevity, commitment, and trust. They could also be described as interdependent, which means they use their romantic partners as a secure base from which they can explore the world. When distressed, they are more likely than an insecure adult to seek comfort from their partner. They are also more likely to give support to their partner when distressed. Moreover, the attributions they make concerning their partner's behavior when they're in conflict tend to alleviate any insecurity. The opposite is true of adults with insecure attachment styles. They make attributions that exacerbate their insecurities.

Insecure Attachment Styles

The two insecure attachment styles (Anxious and Avoidant) involve behaviors that include ambivalence, resistance, and withdrawal. In a way, the child is trying to minimize feelings of attachment and the behaviors that go along with that. They are trying to avoid the pain of having someone they love or need be ripped away from them. They don't want to seem vulnerable. This is confirmed by the research showing that biologically, avoidant children who exhibit behaviors of ambivalence toward their parents following separation are actually experiencing stress. Their heart rate and stress hormone levels are all elevated, even if they appear as cool as a cucumber.

As adults, such individuals are poorly adjusted. Although they can become distressed upon losing someone they love, they are effectively able to dismiss their thoughts and feelings about the loss. They could, in a sense, deactivate their psychological responses to a degree by distracting themselves from attachment-related thoughts. As you might imagine, these individuals come across to their partners as less caring. Additionally, although they can suppress their feelings of losing someone they love, that can create worse problems for themselves in the long run. Insecure attachment styles also result in obsessive behaviors designed to minimize the likelihood of loss. Conflicting emotions and adaptive responses create a kind of push-me-pull-me effect. These individuals are constantly pushing the people they love away, but when they drift too far away, they pull them back in. Of course, extreme attachment disorders can result in a variety of mental disorders, as we've seen through studies.

What Does Attachment Have to Do with Codependency?

So, at an early age, I was neglected by my mother and given responsibilities beyond my years. The latter is often referred to as parentification by the experts, and both of those early childhood experiences are contributing factors to the formation of codependency. But the causes of codependency are multifactorial; various contributors include biological, psychological, and social elements. What's more, codependency can be placed on a spectrum of severity, from excessive feminine (i.e., caretaking) behavior, to that of a behavioral addiction, and all the way to a psychopathological personality disorder. Originally associated with women who, although appearing to dominate their partners, were actually dependent on their spouses, it has come to be recognized as a problem that both men and women can have. Moreover, its occurrence is not just limited to the context of a romantic relationship, and additionally, it's not something that is only the result of early childhood experiences. It can also develop from changes in perception of a woman's role in a sociocultural context, as well as the emergence of a substance abuse problem within the family unit.

Some studies have indicated that children who grow up in homes full of parental conflict—that with alcohol involved or not—can develop codependency in later stages of life. These children learn to put their focus outside of themselves. They learn not to express their feelings for fear of triggering a dysfunctional response from an abusive parent. Furthermore, they embrace the role of "helper" or "savior" within the family. This can easily disrupt their identity development, and as adults, it often creates issues with their partners that can even be viewed as "addictive." As children, they often have attempted to resolve conflicts they witnessed between their parents. They have taken it upon themselves to keep the peace in the family and frequently develop an insecure attachment style that promotes overly dependent interpersonal relationships. What's more, they give up their individual autonomy to serve the needs of the group, which can easily lead to a misrepresentation of reality. They also exhibit poor emotional regulation and insufficient interpersonal communication patterns.

Despite the plethora of symptoms, codependency frequently remains unrecognized. Codependents often enter the health care system complaining of stress-related and depressive symptoms, with the underlying factors remaining invisible. The patient doesn't recognize their own symptoms, nor do they necessarily think that their childhood was in any way problematic. They may see it as normal, since they wouldn't have anything to compare it with.

This was my situation. As part of my child-like adaptive strategy to protect myself from harm, I had convinced myself that my father's acceptance that my mother could never love him was romantic. He loved her that much, despite her love for another man, combined with how he wanted a boy, it all added to my early impression that I was not enough. Still, I grew up thinking my childhood was okay. I wasn't really harmed. Oh, how wrong I was. I didn't see any of the hidden trauma and underlying scars that were accumulating in my life.

My Attachment Style

My attachment style formed when my needs were not met as an infant. Your attachment style forms before you're three years old; in those early years, I could sense my mother's distance, and when she stopped breastfeeding me at only two weeks of age, I learned that sometimes, my need for warmth and closeness might not be met. When my mother became pregnant with my brother and her mother died when I was around six months old, I sensed her distraction and sadness. I also understood at 14 months old that my brother's life and happiness were a clear priority over mine. These experiences contributed to my anxious-avoidant attachment style. As I continued to grow, the experiences of my family life only served to confirm that the world was a dangerous place that didn't care for, nor prioritize, my needs.

I was a calm child and a good girl, but when I was around five to six years old, the Soviet Union collapsed. This was not an easy time for my parents, and at the age of six, we had moved to another town. This is the moment that I later came to realize was when I changed into a shy child who was more reserved and withdrawn. Of course, I had to go to a new school where I didn't know anyone. It was October when we moved, and since it was cold, we weren't allowed to go outside for recess. Thus, I didn't have a chance to make friends on the playground. I was a curious child, so I read a lot.

By the time it was warm again and we could play outside, I hadn't made any real friends, so I was always alone and reading on the balcony. I did finally make a good friend—a girl with whom I could share my secrets and talk about anything—but that wasn't meant to last long. When I was 12 years old, my mother enrolled me in the best humanitarian school in our small town. Once again, I had no one, and once again, I became shy and reserved. Over time, though, I made friends, even though I was never really an excellent student like my mother had been when she was young. That was something she constantly reminded me of, and it was yet another message to say that I simply didn't measure up in her eyes.

Still, I didn't see her behavior as abuse. For me, it was normal. I was proud of my mother's accomplishments in her life, and I loved her. I thought she was the best mother a person could have. I was idealizing her and ignoring her conditional love. When I got good grades, she seemed to love me, but when I didn't, I could see the disappointment in her eyes. I remember when I was around eight or nine years old, I got pretty bad grades in math, and I knew I would have to go home and face her withering disapproval.

I was so sad that I began crying, and I continued crying for hours until I became sick; from there, I got a headache and developed a fever. My shame was manifesting itself in physical symptoms. Somewhere in my psyche, I knew that my mother wouldn't berate me for my bad grades if she saw how much I was suffering. She would, in fact, dedicate herself to caring for me, and that would make me feel special. I remember going to the hospital and feeling so important because it was just her and me there. She was loving and kind, as opposed to her normal way of being—cold, distant, and critical. The somatization I experienced as a result of my emotional distress became my exotic way of avoiding being shamed by my mother for my failures. She believed that criticism was what made a person better, so that's what I remember most from my mother. It was never her support, kind words, or compliments. Then again, I didn't know any better. She was my mother, and like all kids, I saw her as a kind of god that could not be defied or criticized. I tried so hard to be the best so I could get her kind attention, as opposed to her criticism. I wanted her to notice something good in me. I wanted her to see that I was worthy of love.

You can probably see why I developed an insecure attachment style. The early life neglect, combined with a persistent reinforcement of that feeling of neglect left me uncertain of my own worth. My mother's love was conditional, and no matter how hard I worked to please her, I couldn't live up to her expectations. The world did, indeed, feel like a dangerous place that wouldn't provide for my needs.

My mother also groomed me as the helper of the family. My job was to care for my brother at an early age, and I took it upon myself to care for my mother as well. I was constantly hoping that she would recognize my worth and give me the unconditional love I so desperately wanted. This was all part of my developing codependency, and these experiences build upon each other to create a pattern of behavior. At a young age, my pattern was already taking shape.

What About Your Attachment Style?

This is something you might be experiencing as well. You're looking for something, but you aren't even sure what it is. You feel empty, so you question your worth. You want validation, but you don't seem to find it anywhere you look. You want someone to need you, to believe that what you have to offer is a gift they want in their life. You constantly worry about disappointing the people you love because, somewhere deep inside, you are certain that you will eventually. You doubt your abilities, and you invest your time in helping others prove your worth. These are all red flags, but let's dig a little deeper—let's see what lies beneath the surface of these sentiments.

Exercise #1

Reflections on Attachment

In this chapter, I've reflected on some of my childhood experiences and how those contributed to my attachment style and, ultimately, my codependency. Now, I want you to do the same. I have created an exercise to get at the roots of some of your beliefs about yourself and how those might relate to your attachment style. From there, we'll look at the nature of childhood trauma and how it affects psychosocial development. But first, let's do an exercise to identify your attachment style.

Consider the following statements from the time of your earliest childhood memories and rate your experience on a scale of 1 to 5, with 1 being never and 5 being always:

I felt safe with my mother.

Never	Rarely	Sometimes	Usually	Always
1	2	3	4	5

I felt safe with my father.

Never	Rarely	Sometimes	Usually	Always
1	2	3	4	5

My mother encouraged me to explore the world and find my natural talents.

Never	Rarely	Sometimes	Usually	Always
1	2	3	4	5

My father encouraged me to explore the world and find my natural talents.

Never	Rarely	Sometimes	Usually	Always
1	2	3	4	5

My mother was physically present while I was growing up.

Never	Rarely	Sometimes	Usually	Always
1	2	3	4	5

My father was physically present while I was growing up.

Never	Rarely	Sometimes	Usually	Always
1	2	3	4	5

My parents provided for my basic needs (food, housing, and medical care).

Never	Rarely	Sometimes	Usually	Always
1	2	3	4	5

When I was distressed, my parents recognized my distress and made me feel as though they understood how I was feeling.

Never	Rarely	Sometimes	Usually	Always
1	2	3	4	5

When I was distressed, my parents soothed me and calmed me down.

Never	Rarely	Sometimes	Usually	Always
1	2	3	4	5

My parents expressed interest and delight in who I was, and they made me feel valued and loved.

Never	Rarely	Sometimes	Usually	Always
1	2	3	4	5

My parents gave me the material things I wanted to have.

Never	Rarely	Sometimes	Usually	Always
1	2	3	4	5

My parents took me to do the things I wanted to do (activities, visiting friends, etc.)

Never	Rarely	Sometimes	Usually	Always
1	2	3	4	5

I feel comfortable expressing my feelings to my mother (if deceased, rate it based on how you felt when she was alive).

Never	Rarely	Sometimes	Usually	Always
1	2	3	4	5

I feel comfortable expressing my feelings to my father (if deceased, rate it based on how you felt when he was alive).

Never	Rarely	Sometimes	Usually	Always
1	2	3	4	5

I find my mother to be a dependable person.

Never	Rarely	Sometimes	Usually	Always
1	2	3	4	5

I find my father to be a dependable person.

Never	Rarely	Sometimes	Usually	Always
1	2	3	4	5

It helps to turn to my mother in times of need.

Never	Rarely	Sometimes	Usually	Always
1	2	3	4	5

It helps to turn to my father in times of need.

Never	Rarely	Sometimes	Usually	Always
1	2	3	4	5

I worry that my mother doesn't really care for me.

Never	Rarely	Sometimes	Usually	Always
1	2	3	4	5

I worry that my father doesn't really care for me.

Never	Rarely	Sometimes	Usually	Always
1	2	3	4	5

I worry that my mother will abandon me.

Never	Rarely	Sometimes	Usually	Always
1	2	3	4	5

I worry that my father will abandon me.

Never	Rarely	Sometimes	Usually	Always
1	2	3	4	5

Now, time for some reflection: First, add up your score. If you scored 22 - 66, you might have an insecure attachment style. If your score was more than 66, you probably have a secure attachment style. Of course, it would require some work with a therapist to truly understand the nature of your attachment style; a simple test like this can't possibly cover the range of behaviors related to this field. But these questions should give you a rough idea of your basic style. At least, it's a place to reflect on your patterns.

In a personal journal, reflect on your answers. What experiences in your childhood might have made you feel this way? Can you remember specific incidents? Elaborate as much as you like on your answers and the emotions that these memories bring up for you.

Now, let's turn to your romantic partner. If you don't have a current romantic partner, respond to the statements regarding your most recent romantic partner. If you have never had a romantic partner, imagine how you would feel (be brutally honest) about these statements.

I feel comfortable expressing my feelings to this person.

Never	Rarely	Sometimes	Usually	Always
1	2	3	4	5

I find this person to be dependable.

Never	Rarely	Sometimes	Usually	Always
1	2	3	4	5

It helps to turn to this person in times of need.

Never	Rarely	Sometimes	Usually	Always
1	2	3	4	5

I never question whether they care for me—I know they do.

Never	Rarely	Sometimes	Usually	Always
1	2	3	4	5

I never worry about this person abandoning me.

Never	Rarely	Sometimes	Usually	Always
1	2	3	4	5

I can easily calm myself after an argument with this person.

Never	Rarely	Sometimes	Usually	Always
1	2	3	4	5

I can easily show how I'm feeling deep down to this person.

Never	Rarely	Sometimes	Usually	Always
1	2	3	4	5

I know I deserve the love this person gives me.

Never	Rarely	Sometimes	Usually	Always
1	2	3	4	5

Some more scores—add up what you got in this section. If you scored between 8 and 24, that might indicate you don't feel secure in your attachment to this person. Scores above 24 indicate more security in your attachment to your romantic partner. Now, reflect on each of the questions and what they mean. For example, if you answered that you struggle knowing whether you deserve the love this person gives you, what does that say about your concept of self-worth? Why do you think you feel that way? What experiences made you feel that way? Did someone in your life tell you that you don't deserve to be loved? What about your trust in this person—do you trust them, or do you worry about whether they really care about you? Have they given you a reason to distrust them, for example? Can you soothe yourself after an argument with them, or do you want them to comfort you?

People with a secure attachment style generally find it easier to open up to other people and trust them. They are not overly worried about being abandoned, and they feel confident enough in themselves to share their feelings with others. The people in their lives upon whom they were dependent provided for their basic needs, at least most of the time, and were genuinely interested in them. They were present, loving, and soothing when problems arose. They were someone with whom they felt safe. If your answers don't reflect those basic attitudes, it's possible that you have an insecure attachment style, as I do. Again, I would recommend you work with a therapist to uncover the truth about your attachment style and the trauma that created it—but this is still a place to start. If you do appear to have an insecure attachment style, that could lead to codependency or other problems within your relationships and life. It will certainly affect how you view the world in general. But now that you understand more about your attachment style and how it might affect you, you can be better able to deal with your emotions. Let's examine now how childhood trauma can affect your psychosocial development—that's an important part of how you became you.

Chapter 2

Childhood Trauma and Human Psychosocial Development

By now, you may have started to notice some of the elements of my childhood that created an anxious attachment style. I was neglected in my early years, and I was also then parentified—given responsibilities beyond my years when I had to care for my brother. I was constantly criticized and denied unconditional love, which would build a child's self-esteem and encourage healthy identity development. I tried to please my mother, but I was constantly failing to live up to her expectations. These experiences had a dramatic effect on the development of my identity—that is, how I see myself.

This is true for any child. Your experiences early in life will affect how you view your identity and place in the world. Can you identify some of your experiences that affected your development? These will likely be tied to strong memories you have from your younger years. These experiences are foundational for the development of personality, and they are solidly grounded in psychological theory. It's important to understand human psychosocial development theories to understand what happens when things don't proceed healthily.

Erikson's Stages of Human Psychosocial Development

Erik Erikson was a German psychologist who is now considered one of the most influential psychologists of the 20th century. His work in personality development was particularly important. Erikson believed that our personalities develop in a predetermined order through eight stages. These psychosocial development stages occur from infancy through adulthood. In each stage, an individual is faced with a psychosocial crisis, and how that crisis is dealt with can result in a positive or negative outcome. These eight stages, the basic virtues they create if there is a positive outcome, and the age at which they occur are presented in the table below.

Erikson's Eight Stages of Human Psychosocial Development

Stage	Psychosocial Crisis	Basic Virtue	Age

#	Stage	Virtue	Age
1.	Trust vs. Mistrust	Hope	0 - 1½
2.	Autonomy vs. Shame	Will	1½ - 3
3.	Initiative vs. Guilt	Purpose	3 - 5
4.	Industry vs. Inferiority	Competency	5 - 12
5.	Identity vs. Role Confusion	Fidelity	12 - 18
6.	Intimacy vs. Isolation	Love	18 - 40

7.	Generativity vs. Stagnation	Care	40 - 65
8.	Ego Integrity vs. Despair	Wisdom	65+

By understanding what happens in each stage and the possible positive or negative outcomes, you can see how problems in one stage might leave you with certain behavioral patterns, including codependency. Specifically, failure in stages 1, 2, or 3 can result in codependent behavioral patterns, and when you combine that with an insecure attachment style, it makes the likelihood of developing a dependent personality much greater. In my case, my mother was not available to tend to my needs as a newborn. She lost her own mother when I was six months old. Even as an infant, I sensed her sorrow. As a result of her own pain, she was not as responsive to my needs, leaving me to believe that the world was not safe. But I was also left with the trauma of rejection. This kind of trauma forms when you believe people don't care about you or don't love you despite your need or love for them. This early experience caused me to fail to achieve hope in stage 1. Instead, I started to mistrust that my needs would be met, resulting in an insecure (anxious-avoidant) attachment style. This is what ultimately created my form of codependency. I need a lot of love and intimacy from other people, since I didn't get that from my mother. Similarly, I also fell into a pattern of quitting before I got fired out of my fear of rejection, meaning the issue started to leak into other parts of my life.

Stage 1

Trust vs. Mistrust

This is the stage that typically forms your attachment style, as we've discussed. As an infant, you don't know the world yet. You're like an explorer on a distant planet, completely dependent on a caregiver for all your needs. If you get consistent, predictable, and reliable care, you develop a sense of trust. That gives you a strong foundation of security when dealing with challenges later in life. Even if threatened, you will believe you can manage it. A big part of that is developing a virtue of hope. With hope, you can see a better day coming and a better way forward, and you know that you can find that path.

If, on the other hand, you don't get consistent, predictable, or reliable care at this stage, you become fearful. You mistrust your relationships, develop anxiety, feel insecure, and view the world as a more dangerous place. This ties into Bowlby's research on attachment because, with a basic sense of mistrust, you could find it more difficult to develop strong attachments. You don't trust that other people will be there for you and help you. Failing to develop trust at this stage doesn't always mean you've been actively abused by a caregiver. It can happen as a result of neglect or due to processes that are beyond your caregiver's control.

For example, one woman I know was in and out of the hospital during the first two years of her life. This was during a time when her parents were only allowed to visit during visiting hours, which were limited at that time for infants. Moreover, during this time, she was being treated for pneumonia and bronchitis, so she was experiencing a very frightening, unpredictable, painful, and confusing experience as an infant. All she knew was that no one was holding her lovingly very often or consistently, and she was being hurt by needles or other medical equipment. To her, the world was indeed unpredictable, frightening, and painful. While her mother visited her every chance she got and was very loving when she did, it wasn't consistent enough to be predictable. Thus, she developed an insecure attachment style, which naturally bled into her adult relationships.

State 2

Autonomy vs. Shame

This stage of psychosocial development occurs between 18 months and approximately 3 years. It is during this time that a child learns to develop a sense of personal control over their physical abilities, as well as a sense of independence. It's also during this stage that your attachment style forms. If you can do this successfully, you will develop a virtue of will, which will help you become more confident and secure in your abilities. The key to success is if your caregiver encourages you to become independent and supports you in that effort. Although they may let you fail occasionally, the key is that they support and encourage you to try again. They also allow you to be more independent by letting you, for example, walk away from them more, make choices about what you wear, and decide what you eat. They protect you from constant failure, but they also let you learn that you can come back from failure too. If a child's caregivers are critical and overly controlling, or if they prevent them from asserting themselves, the child will come to doubt their abilities. That can cause them to become overly dependent on other people. They will also lack self-esteem and can develop a sense of shame about their inability to do things for themselves.

Stage 3

Initiative vs. Guilt

This stage occurs when the child is about three to five years old, and it is a very rapid period of development. The child is now interacting with other children at school and are playing regularly, which gives them an opportunity to explore their interpersonal skills and initiate activities. They approach and interact with other children, plan activities, and invent games. If they are allowed and encouraged to do this, they will start to gain some confidence in leading others and making decisions for themselves. They develop a sense of initiative. This stage is also when the child will be asking numerous—seemingly endless—questions, and if the caregiver answers them with patience, they are offering a healthy learning environment to the child about the world around them.

Failure in this stage can occur in a number of ways. If a primary caregiver discourages the child's activities and interactions with other children, either due to criticism or from overly controlling their activities, the child will then develop a sense of guilt. Often, a child's behavior during this stage is seen as overly aggressive by a parent, the latter of whom may then punish the child or restrict their activities. This is one way they can cause the child to feel that needless guilt. Additionally, if the caregiver dismisses their questions as stupid, trivial, or embarrassing, the child will feel further guilty and ashamed. With too much guilt, a child's creativity can be inhibited.

Note that some guilt is necessary for the child to learn self-control and have a conscience, but there needs to be a balance. If the child has the right amount of balance between initiative and guilt, then they can feel a purpose, whereas failure can cause an unhealthy amount of guilt.

Stage 4

Industry (Competence) vs. Inferiority

This stage happens between ages five and 12 years old, and it's when children typically learn to read and write, so sums, among other things on their own. Teachers become increasingly more important in the child's life, as do peer groups, and these influences become a major part of how the child builds self-esteem. They want the approval of these people, and they seek it out by demonstrating their competency in performing certain skills. If they can perform well and appropriately according to their peers, family, and teachers, they can gain some pride and more confidence in what they've accomplished.

If their caregiver encourages them and reinforces their initiative, they will start to feel competent or even industrious. They come to believe they can achieve their goals. If they are restricted by parents or teachers, then they will start to doubt their abilities, which can then cause them to not reach their potential. By failing to develop the skills required to be successful in society, they will then start feeling inferior. A little failure can help a child develop modesty, but too much can make them feel incompetent.

Stage 5

Identity vs. Role Confusion

Between 12 to 18 years old, an adolescent starts developing their identity. They are now trying to determine their personal values, beliefs, and goals while transitioning from childhood to adulthood. They are becoming increasingly independent and trying to determine what they want to do with their lives. Do they want a family? What kind of career do they want? How will they fit into society? What will their role be? How they go about answering these questions will end up guiding their ethical development. A healthy outcome for the end of this stage is an integrated sense of self and an understanding of who they are and what they want to be. Success means they grow into the maturational changes that occur in adolescence and are able to accept themselves for who they are. They can also commit to others and accept them, even if there are ideological differences between them, as well as start to take their place in society. Being able to do these things requires the virtue of fidelity.

Of course, to develop their identity, they must explore their possibilities, which means they must be given the freedom to do so by caregivers. Excessive pressure into building a particular identity can result in rebellion, which may then take the form of establishing an unhealthy identity. Without the freedom to explore their environment and opportunities, they may become confused about their role in life. This can make them uncertain about their worth, which can ultimately lead to an unhappy future. Additionally, the failure to develop that sense of identity can lead to numerous psychopathologies, including narcissistic personality disorder and borderline personality disorder. It can cause an individual to have to seek out other people if they want to find their identity, thus eventually leading to a life of dependency on others.

Stage 6

Intimacy vs. Isolation

This stage occurs in the prime of life—that is, between the ages of 18 and 40 years old. The conflict that happens during this time is usually centered around forming loving relationships with other people. People in this age range share themselves more intimately with others while exploring relationships that might lead to long-term commitments outside of the family. If an individual is successful and able to be intimate with others, they can form happy relationships based on commitment, safety, and mutual care. On the other hand, if they are unable to get close to others, then they come to fear commitment and may be unable to form long-lasting, healthy relationships. This can lead to isolation, loneliness, and other problems like depression and anxiety. Success during this stage is imperative to ensure loving and healthy relationships.

Stage 7

Generativity vs. Stagnation

This stage occurs between the age of 40 and 65 years old, and it is a period often called "making your mark." This is when people think about how they will be remembered and what they will leave behind. People in this stage often wish to nurture or create something they consider meaningful and beneficial to other people. These are the things people will remember about them. It's a way to give back to the world. You might do this by raising good children, becoming successful in your career, and/or getting involved with your community. Generativity means that the person feels like they are a part of something bigger than themselves. They feel useful and accomplished, leading to the virtue of care. If they are not successful, they feel stagnant, unproductive, and as though they only have a shallow connection to the world around them. They feel disconnected and uninvolved with their community and their culture.

Stage 8

Ego Integrity vs. Despair

Erikson's final stage of psychosocial development begins at age 65 and ends with death. This is when an individual contemplates their accomplishments, reflects on their life, takes note of any regrets, and, if successful, accepts their life as something that was meant to be. This makes them feel coherent and whole, knowing they led a successful life. Their productivity at this stage slows down, and they can retire in peace. As they have developed the virtue of wisdom, they believe they can die without fear. Although they may occasionally feel some despair, it is balanced by their ego integrity and doesn't overcome them. On the other hand, if a person feels unproductive, guilty about what they've done in their past, or that they didn't accomplish the things they wanted to do in life, they may feel a profound despair that they cannot overcome. They will be dissatisfied with their life, which can lead to depression and hopelessness, given that there's little they believe they can do about it all now.

Back to My Story

From my story so far, it's easy to see that I experienced mistrust in Stage 1 due to my mother's critical nature and tendency to control and saddle me with too much responsibility. Given this state of affairs, it is logical that I rebelled in my teenage years. While my parents were merely okay together, they did have their fights. I always sided with my mother, of course, because I saw my father as someone who wasn't as good as her. I thought he should feel lucky that she was with him. Well, maybe that message had been transmitted to me over the years from my mother.

But he worked very hard to take care of our family and live up to my mother's expectations. After all, he was working under the burden of knowing that she didn't really love him, so I can't blame him for wanting to imagine a different reality or avoid it altogether from time to time. He would go out with his friends and really tie one on. Usually, when this happened, my mother would welcome him home with a veritable deluge of accusations and comments about morality and how he wasn't demonstrating any. They would often fight for half the night. Of course, my mother always painted herself as a victim, martyr, and saint, and I always took her side. In fact, I loved her even more when she was complaining about my father. As a child, I had seen him as a terrible man, but that was the drama created in my family, often by my mother herself.

On one occasion, my mother didn't get up and fight with my father when he came home drunk. Instead, she pretended to be asleep as a way of punishing him with her silence and indifference. He was a man who wanted her acceptance, love, and respect, so he would get lonely without any response from her. He decided to take a bath to calm himself, but he fell asleep in the tub. A few days later, he became ill with bilateral pneumonia. He was hospitalized and treated for more than a year, and although he survived, he was always weak after that experience, and after, he was ultimately diagnosed with liver cancer and only lived for seven more years. It was during my teenage years that he was in the hospital, always hovering between life and death. During his treatment and after he died, our family suffered financially since my mother's salary was so low, making it very difficult to survive. We often didn't even have enough money for food, and we additionally had to pay the medical bills for my father.

As you might imagine, my mother was constantly irritated by this situation. She was moody and quick to fly into a rage. I couldn't even find refuge at school. We didn't have enough money for clothing and shoes, so I was ridiculed for my appearance by my peers. It was a really tough time for all of us. By the time I was ready to enter the university, I couldn't wait to get away from this terrible, small town and the tyranny of my mother's abuse. She constantly made accusations and devalued me. I was yearning to be free and independent. What's more, when I was 16 years old, I had a terrible experience that would affect my ability to develop intimate, long-lasting, committed relationships, but I will elaborate on that in the next chapter. Right now, let's talk about you.

Exercise #2

How Did You Do in Each Stage?

This exercise will help you reflect on how you fared in these stages of psychosocial development. Begin by answering the following questions, but be aware that you may experience a variety of emotions while doing so. You may feel rage, sadness, fear, among many other emotions that you might not expect. This is why it's vital that you take care of yourself throughout the process. Be kind to yourself, particularly if you uncover certain memories where a caregiver may have failed you. Remember that no matter what you experienced, you survived, and you are stronger and more resilient than you realize because of it. Make sure you have someone you love and who has your best interests at heart ready to respond to a call for help. Also, make sure you treat yourself with the kindness, love, and respect you deserve. With that in mind, let's proceed. After each question, elaborate and reflect on your thoughts, experiences, and emotions in your journal. Remember, there are no wrong answers here; this exercise is for self-exploration, so be honest with yourself.

- **Question #1:** What do you know about your infancy? Were your caregivers present, or were there periods of separation?
- **Question #2:** Do you feel a need to always develop a contingency plan when making decisions? In other words, do you need a Plan A, Plan B, Plan C, etc.?
- **Question #3:** Do you fear that you will have needs that won't be met? Has this ever happened to you?
- **Question #4:** Do you often feel helpless? What kinds of situations make you feel helpless?
- **Question #5:** Do strange situations or environments frighten and make you retreat?

- **Question #6:** Do you like to travel to places you've never been to before?
- **Question #7:** Do you believe that you make a positive contribution to your family, community, and culture?
- **Question #8:** If someone you love is better at something than you are, do you feel proud of them?
- **Question #9:** Do you feel proud when you can do something well?
- **Question #10:** Do you know your role in society?
- **Question #11:** Are you confident that you know who you are, what your values are, and what your beliefs are?
- **Question #12:** Are you comfortable being vulnerable around someone you love?

The following questions are for people over 40 years of age.

- **Question #13:** What are some things you've done in your life that you believe are beneficial to others?
- **Question #14:** In what ways do you make positive contributions to your community?
- **Question #15**: Are you a good friend?

The following questions are for people over 65 years of age.

- **Question #16:** Do you have any regrets? If so, what are they?
- **Question #17**: What accomplishments are you most proud of?
- **Question #18:** Do you believe the things that happened in your life happened for a reason?
- **Question #19:** Do you believe the challenges you faced in life made you stronger?
- **Question #20:** If you were to die today, would you feel like you had done everything you came here to do?

Once you have answered these questions, take a look at your answers and what they say about the different stages of your life. How do you think you fared in each stage of psychosocial development? What kinds of experiences affected your outcomes in each stage? Reflect on these findings in your journal and be sure to treat yourself to an act of kindness after you finish this exercise. Go do something you like, eat something you love, and show yourself a little love. Now that you have a better understanding of your development, let's look a little deeper into the psychology of codependency.

Chapter 3

The Psychology of Codependency

I was 16 years old, and my life was in a constant state of chaos. My father was hovering between life and death, and my mother was constantly irritated. School was a nightmare, where I was ridiculed for my appearance and how I never had enough money for me to dress to the standards of my peers. I felt awkward and unaccepted everywhere I turned. No matter how hard I tried, I couldn't seem to please anyone—well, almost anyone. There was a man, the director of our gymnasium, who showered me with affection. He was 50 years old and always all smiles and compliments. He was flirting, but I didn't see it as a young, naive girl. I get it now, but at the time, I didn't know. He seemed at times to be my only friend, and I was starved for affection. This man wanted me to go to one of the best universities in our country. He even met my mother to convince her to support me in applying to this university. Well, she decided that he was attracted to her, and her eyes had quite the shine when she told me about it. She was practically gushing. The problem was, it wasn't her whom he was interested in.

The next day, he called me into his office. Everything happened so fast. All of sudden, his hands were under my dress, touching my thighs and bum, and his lips were kissing my neck and making their way down my body. I didn't know what to do, so I just ran away from him and his office; I was lucky to get away. After that, I didn't know what to do. I remember sitting in the shower the next morning and just crying. I knew I couldn't tell my mother because I knew she would never believe he found me attractive over her. He was a very well-respected man in our small town, so I knew I couldn't go to the police. I knew that no one would believe me. What's more, if I was to have any chance of getting into that university, I had to graduate from this school—and his gymnasium—normally. I couldn't change my school in the last year of my time there. But it was still eight more long months until graduation. That's a long time to avoid a man intent on raping you. The only person I told about this was my friend. She was the only shoulder I had to cry on.

I also knew I was in trouble, so I told my mother that the university in the city nearest to us was fine with me instead. Somehow—I'm not sure how—the whole situation got resolved. He didn't stop trying to be alone with me, but I managed to dodge his attempts to rape me. I fear many other girls in my school were not so lucky, but I was not among them. I told my mother 20 years after it had happened, and you know what? She didn't believe me. She couldn't believe that someone would choose me over her.

This was the reality of my adolescence. If we look back at Erikson's stages of psychosocial development, we can see that during this time of my life, I was developing my identity. Failure to develop an integrated identity results in role confusion, and with a constantly critical mother, an ailing, distant father figure, and a lack of acceptance among my peers, the addition of a traumatic event like an attempted rape only further complicated the situation. You can understand how this would make me question my self-worth and cause difficulties in accepting myself for who I am. In fact, I didn't really know who I was or what my purpose in life would be. **How about you? Can you identify a stage where you might have not experienced the ideal outcome?** To really understand how this kind of dysfunctional family environment can affect personality structure and organization, we have to delve a little deeper into transactional analysis and personality organization.

Understanding the Levels of Personality Organization

Otto Kernberg was an Austrian-American psychoanalyst who identified several levels of personality organization. These are the following:

- Psychotic Personality Organization
- Borderline Personality Organization
- Neurotic Personality Organization
- Mature Personality Organization

Kernberg wanted to identify how personality organization progresses to better understand personality disorders. He wanted to understand how our psyche develops. He based his categories on the types and use of psychological defense mechanisms, the extent to which an individual is able to perceive reality, one's identity integration, awareness and control of aggression, and to what extent they are guided by moral ideals and values. Initially, we all start out with primitive defense mechanisms, like projecting our unflattering qualities onto other people. We don't use more mature defense mechanisms, like rationalization. Likewise, we are prone to "magical thinking:" we are initially unable to differentiate self from non-self, control our aggression, or really have a moral code. As we grow and learn from our parents and society, we progress from these primitive mechanisms of defense; we increasingly learn to cast aside our magical thinking, adopt morals, and learn who we are. We move into the borderline spectrum within about two years in response to our early life circumstances. Between three to six years old is when most people move into the neurotic level of personality organization. This is when children learn about guilt and shame. Typically, we reach the mature level at approximately 25 years old. This is how our personality organizes; however, trauma in the form of abuse or neglect can stifle that progression. When that happens, a person may be stuck at a so-called more primitive level of personality organization; with severe trauma, they can even regress to a previous level. Let's explore each level to better understand the characteristics of each and how that level can affect our behavior.

Psychotic Personality Organization

This is where we all start as infants. This is the least healthy level of personality organization, and it includes people with severely disorganized personalities. People in this category have poorly compromised reality testing, meaning they may hear or see things that are not present, or they may believe they have special powers or are receiving special messages. They also have an inconsistent sense of self and others, and they use extremely immature defense mechanisms when stressed. These individuals don't have a concept of themselves as distinct from other people. Therefore, they have difficulty determining experiences and perceptions that come from their own mind as opposed to others or their environment. They can't cope well at all with stress, and they don't function well in society. Although some of this thinking may be normal in an infant, it becomes pathological in older individuals.

Borderline Personality Organization

You may have heard of Borderline Personality Disorder, and although this level of personality organization includes people with BPD, they are not the same thing. In this level, reality testing is mostly intact, but they have a fragmented sense of self and others. In a normal progression, this typically occurs in response to life experiences encountered during the first two years of life. But with trauma, a person can get stuck at this level. Their sense of self remains fragmented. That means they don't have a consistent view of themselves or others across situations and over time. For example, emotionally mature people can be angry at someone but still identify that person as good and love them. People with a fragmented self identity and inability to recognize others' have difficulty maintaining positive feelings about people when they're angry at them. This is because, in part, they tend to see people as extensions of their own identity. They can't see people as mixtures of bad and good; instead, they think in binary terms: you're either all good or all bad. This is known as splitting, and it's a common primitive defense mechanism employed by people with this kind of personality organization. As you might imagine, this can create numerous repetitive problems in their interpersonal relationships. All of this translates into recurring issues, which can involve problems like substance abuse, obesity, dependence, and toxic partners.

Neurotic Personality Organization

These individuals are similar to those with a mature personality organization, in that they have intact reality testing, a good sense of self and others, and a fairly good understanding of what their life goals are. Most people move into this level between three and six years of age, when they first encounter feelings like guilt or shame. This is the beginning of recognizing that there are consequences for one's actions. From here, healthy individuals continue to mature. Those who don't get stuck at an earlier level usually have a more consistent direction and understanding of their purpose. They are able to form strong, committed relationships and can view other people more accurately. They are mostly successful at coping with stress effectively, but they tend to use neurotic defense mechanisms like repression to deal with stressful situations. This is the main difference between this personality organization and that of a mature personality organization. They have a secure attachment style, but they may not have experienced success at every level of Erikson's human psychosocial development.

Mature Personality Organization

This is the healthiest level of personality organization, and in a normal progression, individuals reach this level by approximately 25 years of age. People with mature personality organizations have more reliable defense mechanisms when things go wrong. These include using humor to process stressful situations. They may also use something like anticipation to work out the logical consequences of various behaviors. People with this type of personality organization also have a well-integrated sense of self, as well as healthy representations of "other." They additionally have good reality testing capabilities. Basically, this person is well-adjusted with respect to their identity and the world around them. They would also have a secure attachment style and would have experienced the ideal outcomes associated with each stage of psychosocial development.

In general, the mature and neurotic levels of personality organization are at the healthier end of the spectrum, whereas the borderline and psychotic levels are at the more disordered end of the spectrum. Those with borderline and psychotic personality organizations would have insecure attachment styles, and they would have failed to achieve optimal outcomes in several stages of psychosocial development. They have a fragmented recognition of their identity and think in polarized patterns of all good or all bad. They often change careers, romantic partners, and life goals very rapidly and haphazardly; this is an incredibly painful way to live.

So Where Does Codependency Fit Into the Picture?

Everyone is dependent to some degree, and everyone needs a little help from their friends and family from time to time. But sometimes, that need can become excessive to the degree that the dependent person becomes clingy or *craves* that connection with other people. They may become submissive in an attempt to get their needs met, and they may even humiliate themselves in that regard. However, dependency is not just an individual state; all cultures encourage some level of dependency. Some within a culture may be denied their personal autonomy. For example, the very young, the very old, sick people, and criminals are all people whom our culture, and virtually every other culture, will make legally dependent on some authority. It's only when such dependency doesn't conform to sociocultural norms that it becomes pathological. Codependency is a condition that shares many overlapping symptoms with Dependent Personality Disorder (DPD). The distinction between the two is found in the nature of the dependent relationship. Codependents focus their dependency traits on a specific person, whereas people with

DPD display dependent traits toward others in general. The difference is really of degree rather than kind.

Codependency is when someone becomes highly dependent on someone in their life. Their dependence is so complete that their self-esteem and identity are negatively affected, and they identify themselves *with* that dependency. They are constantly preoccupied with over-the-top worries, and their fear of abandonment paralyzes them. This turmoil makes them indecisive, and even simple decisions end up beyond their capacity. For that reason, they usually won't initiate projects or events on their own. Their fears, coupled with indecisiveness, cause them to seek reassurance repeatedly from everyone around them. In essence, they are handing over responsibility for their own life to other people. They don't trust themselves to be responsible for their own happiness. They have delegated that responsibility to other people in their lives. Then, by dedicating themselves to ensuring others are happy and satisfied, they can then find their own happiness through them. In short, codependents love themselves by loving someone else so intensely that they give themselves over to that person.

Another quality that codependents lack is an inner compass. They can't realistically assess their own positive qualities, and because they have limited their life by dedicating it to someone else. Those limitations force them to be reliant on input from elsewhere. That causes them to be fearful of losing the support they get from those outside sources. They can't disagree with or criticize them since they are reliant on their support. Consequently, they cater to the needs of the people to whom they have dedicated themselves. They were taught to behave this way as a child. Their parents taught them only to expect conditional, transactional love. If they behave well and provide what their parents want from them, they will be rewarded with their love. This unjust treatment can cause a rage in the child, and they then may either direct that rage inwardly, producing a masochist or a depressive illness, or outwardly, resulting in psychopathy. Like their rage, their love can be directed inwardly, contributing to narcissism, or outwardly, contributing to codependence.

In the case of codependence, the individual who suffers from this seeks to merge with their love object. In that way, they can love themselves by providing love to the object of their affection. This dependence becomes the affected individual's comfort zone—their best friend in a way. The individual who exhibits codependency is both fixated on and reliant upon their state of dependence. It's a difficult trap to extract oneself from because it disguises itself as love. You tell yourself that you're only doing what you're doing because it's a demonstration of your love. The problem is that you don't truly love yourself, and you're trying to fill that void by pouring your love into someone else. The need is so strong that you start to believe you can't live without your dependence, which you see incarnate in the person to whom you're addicted. It's a dysfunctional pattern of behavior in relationships; it's learned, and it's something a child witnesses in parental interactions. Fortunately, the positive aspect behind all this is that it is acquired knowledge, and therefore, this behavior can be unlearned.

The Realization of My Codependence

After I left for university, I came upon some very difficult times. I had to survive all alone in a big city, and sometimes, I didn't even have enough money for dinner. I would have to walk home from university because I didn't have the money to pay for transportation. Still, I felt happy; I thought I was doing okay. I was away from my mother's harsh criticism and the difficulties of life at home. I felt happy inside without all of the fighting and complaining. I survived those lean times, graduated with my degree, and ended up young and successful. I had opened my own little business, had a car and an apartment, and did my best to take care of my mother by buying her new clothes and sending her on vacation every year. I thought it would make her proud of me.

My father died right after I graduated. I organized his funeral, but I couldn't stop blaming him for getting sick. I kept thinking that if he had stayed healthy, I wouldn't have had to suffer the hardships I did while in school. I also thought he could have protected me from the troubles I had in my young life.

At that time, I was not choosing my relationships; the men in my life were choosing me because of my looks and success. As you can see by how I was still devoted to taking care of my mother and blaming my father for my problems, I was fully codependent at that time. The years of my mother's harsh criticism and my father's neglect had taught me that love was conditioned on my performance. I had also been taking care of someone from a very early age—first my brother, then my mother and father. I had turned that love outward and invested it in external sources of validation. I needed to pour my love into someone so I could then love myself vicariously. I jumped from one codependent relationship to another in my romantic partners. By 33, I was divorced for a second time. I had married a narcissist—a familiar kind of relationship—and I was left feeling completely empty and horribly depressed. If you would like to read more about this turning point in my life, I have written another book on the topic: *My Toxic Husband: Loving and Breaking Up with a Narcissistic Man—Start Your Psychopath-free Life Now!* This experience was when I started to realize that there was something wrong with me. I couldn't see it because, remember, it's easy to convince ourselves that our codependency is just an expression of our loving nature. But I knew that I couldn't seem to have a normal relationship, and without that, I would never have the family I had always dreamed of having. I had to analyze the reasons behind my poor decision-making processes and find ways to modify them. And so, I started psychotherapy.

Exercise #3

Your Codependence

Codependency is not a distinct personality disorder recognized by the DSM-5, but it shares many overlapping symptoms with Dependent Personality Disorder.

Reflect on the following diagnostic criteria for DPD and on whether they are true for you. Although this is not a true diagnosis, it can help you determine your patterns of behavior:

- All-consuming, unrealistic fear of being abandoned.
- Anxiety or feelings of helplessness when alone.
- Inability to manage life responsibilities without seeking help from others.
- Problems stating an opinion out of fear of losing support or approval.
- Strong drive to get support from others, even choosing to do unenjoyable things to get it.
- Trouble making everyday decisions without input or reassurance from others.
- Trouble starting or completing projects due to a lack of self-confidence or ability to make decisions.
- Urge to seek a new relationship for support and approval when a close relationship ends.

If you have checked yes to five or more of these criteria, and if you focus your dependency traits on one person rather than everyone in general, you're likely codependent. Now, think about some of the symptoms of codependency, such as avoiding personal responsibility, difficulty being alone, being overly sensitive to criticism, lacking self-confidence, and having difficulty with everyday decisions. Contemplate your early years to identify the root cause of these symptoms. Try to think of the first time you felt any of them. For example, when was the first time you felt fearful of being alone? When was the first time you believed you couldn't make a simple decision without input from someone else? Attempt to recollect instances from your childhood where you believed you lacked the ability to perform tasks independently or that you were insufficient. This might have been because of a critical parent—as was my case—or it may have come from an offhand comment made by someone you admire. Whatever the situation, write down your thoughts and feelings about that memory in your journal. Writing it down will help you recognize the origins of your problem. This is where we begin. We must understand the nature of the problem before we can seek treatment for it. Rage on the page to release some of that pent-up negative emotion that helped form your dependency. Then, take five deep breaths, and let yourself know that you love yourself, and it's time to begin that healing journey.

Chapter 4

The Signs of Relationship Addiction

I discovered through my own healing journey that an overriding core belief I had adopted about myself was that I was not enough. I had learned my place in childhood and had been told that I was nothing special. I was not ugly, nor beautiful. I was not stupid, nor smart. I was plain, average, and nothing to write home about. When other people would tell me I was beautiful, I just thought they were being polite. Even after all the years of therapy, my education in the field of psychology, and my practice as a psychotherapist, I still sometimes struggle with my internal support mechanisms and confidence. Every time I believe I've overcome my past, I hear my mother accusing or devaluing me. Although I no longer consciously accept those negative statements, her abuse was something that I incorporated as part of my core identity. It's [something often referred to as introjection](), and for many, it typically occurs in the first three years of life.

Introjection and the Mother-Child Relationship

Introjection is the opposite of projection. Projection is when someone else projects their own feelings or characteristics onto another person. Introjection, however, happens when you internalize the beliefs, emotions, attitudes, etc., of other people. It's very common between children and their parents—particularly their mother—and although it occurs throughout your development, it is most pronounced between the ages of three and six years of age, when a child wants to be an adult, and of course, they want to be like their mother or father. When you introject, you identify with another person so strongly that you can't separate yourself from them. What's even more insidious is that introjection happens without a lot of thought. In fact, it can happen without any thought whatsoever. When a newborn infant sees the face of a loving, supportive, and comforting mother, they introject those attitudes, and that stays with them throughout their life. If, on the other hand, a newborn infant is met with a mother's face that is irritated, neglectful, and projecting negative emotions and thoughts, that infant introjects those attitudes. The infant isn't analyzing them; they are simply accepting them as part of their reality and part of their identity.

Introjections are also not something you can access consciously. These are attitudes you've adopted and accepted as true. You don't have a distinct memory of being told something or something happening to you. You just have a vague feeling of either positivity or negativity.

For those with positive experiences of introjection, you adopt certain traits such as compassion, loyalty, and morality. Of course, these can be very helpful during difficult times. You don't consciously think about them; you simply feel them pervasively and intensely. To give you an example, if you introjected positive traits from your mother as an infant, and someone tells you that you're "just like your mother," you would experience happy, vivid, and warm feelings and memories. It's almost like she's a spirit inside your head emanating love for you.

If, on the other hand, you introjected negative traits or emotions from your mother as an infant, you may feel a pervasive sense of worthlessness. You can't put your finger on exactly why that would be, but you feel incompetent, guilty, or inept. You may also find it difficult to readily discover and form a strong identity. As you grow older, you start to lack self-confidence, and you also develop a negative internal voice or dialogue. You become your unloving, critical mother. She's like a scary ghost living in your head, filling you with self-doubt and low self-worth. What's even worse is that you won't know that it came from her. One client realized she had introjected her mother's outright contempt for her as an infant. It left her believing that not only was she not enough, but she was also undeserving of anything good. She related a story about a computer she recently bought that wasn't working well. It was brand new, and still, it wasn't working as it should. That's frustrating in general, but for her, it was devastating, and she couldn't quite put her finger on why. When she analyzed it further, she realized that she had introjected her mother's negative feelings toward her to the extent that she had a pervasive belief that nothing would ever work out for her, even something as simple as a computer working normally. Does this story resonate with you at all? Think about what your pervasive beliefs are. You usually encounter them when you're frustrated like that client.

You can similarly introject negative or positive traits from your father. I had a client who had introjected her father's assessment of her as a "real shit." She carried that image of herself inside for many years without fully realizing how it got there. It was like a secret name she had given herself, but it really came from her father. Although you might surpass the criticism you remember receiving from your parents, you may be unable to shake the feeling of inadequacy that you internalized during infancy. This is what happened to me. When I was old enough to remember my mother's critical statements, I had already introjected that worthlessness, to where her criticisms only seemed like valid justification for what I already felt inside.

Though I no longer accept my mother's criticisms and devaluation, the dark shadow of introjection still haunts me. That's why I hear her voice in my head telling me I'm worthless, wrong, and undeserving of happiness. That's why it took me almost 40 years to clean out the wounds of the trauma she inflicted on me my entire life. It's the trauma of rejection—something reflected even in her recent remarks, where she asked me how my current husband could bear to live with me. She also told me that she couldn't understand what he saw in me; this isn't the first time she's said this kind of thing about a man in my life.

While I used to take those criticisms to heart, I now at least recognize them for the abuse they are. This is part of what created my need to please others in order to love myself. I tried for so many years to pour my love into my mother, so I could feel loved vicariously through her. I wanted her acceptance and love. I wanted her to see me and think that I was special, at least to her. That never happened, but it left a dark legacy: my codependency. Let us delve deeper into the various categories of codependency to gain a better understanding.

Codependent Types

Codependency is a complex problem. It is a multi-faceted defense mechanism designed to protect the codependent from their own fears and needs. They've been taught that they don't matter except as related to how they can care for others. But that manifests in different ways that are related to specific etiologies of the problem. There are five categories of codependence. Let's take a closer look at each one.

- ❖ **Codependency Designed to Alleviate Fear of Abandonment**

Codependency that develops to alleviate fears of abandonment produces people who are clingy, smothering, and often panic. They exhibit self-negating submissiveness in the hope that they can prevent their loved ones from leaving them. They also don't want to attain any level of true autonomy or independence. They merge with their loved ones, and if they perceive signs of abandonment, whether real or imagined, they see that as a kind of self-annihilation. It is literally as if they are abandoning themselves or as if a part of them is dying. As a result, they are not above using emotional blackmail and threats to force their victims to comply with what they want.

❖ Codependency to Cope with a Fear of Losing Control

This type of codependent feigns helplessness to get those around them to cater to their needs and desires. They appear as drama queens, and their lives are of almost constant instability and chaos. These individuals never grow up, and they utilize self-imputed deficiencies and disabilities as weapons to force their loved ones to treat them as emotional and/or physical invalids. They will also use blackmail and threats to force compliance with their wishes.

❖ Vicarious Codependents

Just as you might imagine, these are codependents who live vicariously through others. They live in the shadow of their targets and bask in the glow of their reflected glory. They see themselves as the "woman behind the man" or the "man behind the woman." They imagine that it's really their support and love that allows their target to thrive. As the song goes, they see themselves as "the wind beneath the wings" of their target. They suspend their lives and desires in favor of supporting those of their loved one, and they see that sacrifice as their greatest accomplishment.

❖ Oscillating Codependents

This codependent is often also called a codependent or borderline narcissist. They oscillate between periods when they exhibit codependent behaviors, like being extremely clingy, and periods when they are more aloof, detached, and neglectful. When they're exhibiting codependent behaviors, they interpret those as intimacy, and when they're aloof, they view themselves as reclaiming their personal space. They will also sometimes form a shared psychosis with their intimate partners. This is something known as *folie à deux*, and in its extreme form, it's been seen in cases of pairs of serial killers, such as the Hillside Stranglers and Leonard Lake and Charles Ng.

In milder cases, it usually manifests as a loss of autonomy for both partners. The reason behind it is the all-consuming fear of abandonment. That's also true for the aloof oscillation. The idea behind this is that the codependent individual is quitting before they get fired. They abandon their intimate partner to preserve an illusion of control over the situation. Another common feature of this codependency type is something known as coextensivity. This is where codependent individuals expect their partners to read their minds. They believe their intimacy should allow them to intuit each other's thoughts, emotions, and moods. This type of codependent will also use shifting boundaries to create dependence in their partner. They become behaviorally unpredictable to confuse their partners and keep them guessing.

❖ Counterdependents

The last category is one that has only been identified recently. It's that of counterdependents. These are individuals who despise authority and will clash with authority figures, such as their parents, boss, and the police. It's in these acts of defiance that this type of codependent derives their self-identity. They are uncompromisingly independent, but they are also controlling, self-centered, and even aggressive. They force other people to affirm their view of the world and expectations. Because of their fiercely independent nature, they are extremely fearful of intimacy, which makes them feel as though they are being held captive. This causes them to be bad team players. They consider themselves to be lone wolves, yet they engage in approach-avoidance repetition compulsion cycles. This is where they are hesitant to approach others and become engaged in close relationships. That is followed by a fear and avoidance of any level of commitment. This type of codependent doesn't just fear their own weaknesses; they actually dread them. They may compensate for that by projecting an image of being omnipotent, omniscient, or superior. That might sound like narcissism to you—and in fact, most overt or grandiose narcissists are counterdependent. They have buried their emotions and needs under layers of scar tissue that formed as a result of the abuse they endured as a child. They use their grandiosity as a shield against their insecurity, shame, and self-loathing.

Situational Codependence

It is also possible that some may develop codependent behaviors in the wake of a life crisis. Many who go through a divorce or some other form of abandonment may begin to exhibit codependent behaviors. When this happens, the person usually experiences a complex set of emotions, the role of which is to resolve the inner turmoil they are experiencing as a result of undesirable codependent behaviors. For example, someone may be dumped by their romantic partner, and initially, they may feel liberated. But the abandonment leaves them feeling lonesome and somewhat disoriented subconsciously. This can cause them to rush into a new relationship before fully grieving the old one and without fully vetting the new one. On some level, the person has always dreaded being lonely, but with no real solution to being abandoned so suddenly, the individual suppresses these feelings and is unable to cope with them. When left alone, that suppressed dread reemerges, and it causes the person to engage in codependent behaviors to avoid being left alone ever again. The codependence, in this case, is a dysfunctional defense mechanism designed to fend off abandonment.

Because this kind of person often has a balanced and strong sense of self, they are unhappy with their codependent behavior because they have always seen themselves as strong and confident with a well-regulated sense of self-worth. This new part of their behavior is frustrating—it runs counter to their self-image, and they dedicate themselves to getting rid of these unbecoming behaviors.

To get rid of them, the person subconsciously chooses someone who is not right for them, then goes about proving to themselves that this person is wrong for them before discarding that person. By taking control of the situation, they are reestablishing their autonomy, and they can then be assured that they are rid of their codependency.

Situational codependency can be characterized by a suppressed, underlying fear of abandonment. It hides until awakened by some life crisis, such as a divorce, an empty nest, or the death of a loved one. At first, the individual may feel exhilarated with their new-found freedom, but that doesn't last, and it actually may enhance their anxiety. The person might even worry about their finding this freedom intoxicating and choose to remain alone for the rest of their life. They are also plagued by nagging fears that they need to find someone quickly; they're not getting any younger, after all. They develop situational codependence to cope with the internal turmoil it causes. As a result, they quickly attract an intimate partner to forestall their abandonment. But most situational codependents tend to be ego-dystonic. That means they look inward to determine the problem and examine their dissatisfaction. Because their codependence is so contrary to their true nature, they reestablish their autonomy by getting rid of the new partner. The person may not be aware of these internal dynamics.

My Type of Codependence

My mother was the product of her upbringing, generation, and environment, as is true of anyone. She was subjected to her own trauma, which caused her to develop in very narcissistic ways unconsciously. As a result, she created a dysfunctional family environment that was chaotic and unsupportive as an adult. She was jealous of her daughter—as is true of any narcissistic mother—and she made her son into a golden child, which is also typical. Because of her jealousy, she constantly devalued and blamed me for anything that went wrong, but in her mind, she was making me stronger. Although she may have been doing the best she could, given her own trauma, she also had unrealistic expectations for me and parentified me at a young age. Like most children in that kind of dysfunctional family environment, I always assumed the problem was me. And my mother manipulated me to ensure I believed that for her own reasons. I learned that love was conditional and dependent upon my good behavior, a goal that shifted constantly. My mother was seeking to undermine my self-esteem, self-confidence, and self-worth, perhaps because she believed I might otherwise become too vain. I desired her approval, and so I continued to give in the futile hope that someday, she would see, accept, and love me. Her approval became my source of self-esteem. Her blame-shifting caused me to feel guilty and somehow responsible for things that were clearly beyond my control. Because I felt responsible and couldn't seem to do anything correctly, I felt worthless; I was not enough. It's important to understand that I'm not blaming her, *per se*, for I do believe that what happened has made me a better person. By understanding the legacy of intergenerational trauma, we can finally break the cycle. It's not about hating or blaming a parent for your problems; it's about understanding their origins so you can grow into the best possible version of yourself.

As a child, I lacked the cognitive abilities and life experience to understand that how my mother treated me wasn't healthy. I just thought that this was the way everyone's mother acted. Every child thinks that way about their family. Your family is the norm in your mind because it's all you know. Because my self-worth was firmly rooted in my mother's approval, my coping strategy became one of trying to please her. That became a pattern that followed me into adulthood. I sought intimate, familiar partners because they treated me like my mother had. I continued to try to please them to feel loved. I was trying to love myself by pouring my devotion into my partner and basking in the glow of their gratitude. Because I was picking dysfunctional partners, however, there never was any gratitude—just like there never was any gratitude from my mother. I was a vicarious codependent looking for love in all the wrong places. I was looking for love through my relationships with other people. But my fear of rejection also created elements of oscillating codependency. I would often invent a reason to break off a relationship so I could avoid the pain of rejection later on. The problem, however, was with my relationship with myself. This illustrates the complexity of codependency; no one fits into a single, neat category. There are often overlapping elements in codependent types.

It's only been within the last couple of years that I closely examined why my mother treated me the way she did. I can sometimes see something that looks like love for me in her eyes, but it never shows in how she treats me. That's because to show her love would make her vulnerable, and as a narcissist, she couldn't let herself do that. I used to be angry about this, but now I'm just sorry. I'm sorry for her and her mental condition. I'm sorry for the child I was who never got the love she deserved. I'm sorry that I spent so much time in my life blaming myself for something that was not my fault. I'm sorry that it took me so long to figure out that I deserved love just for being me. I'm sorry for these things, but I'm grateful too. I'm grateful that I was able to discover why I now engage in these patterns of behavior. I'm grateful that I have found my true self-worth. I'm grateful for the gifts my childhood gave me. It was hard, but I survived, and I survived because I am resilient. I'm grateful that I have found new, healthier coping strategies for dealing with life's challenges, those challenges also including toxic people. I'm grateful that I am now giving myself the unconditional love that my mother should have given me. In this way, my criticizing, distant mother gave me the power I needed to fight for the best life I could have and prove that I could not only heal, but also thrive. My pain created my power, and this is true of any traumatizing event. It's a cliche, but what doesn't kill you truly does make you stronger if you search for that which suffering has brought to you. Think about your own situation and how the problems you've faced in life have made you stronger. What did you learn from them, and how have you used that to prove to your parents or the world that you can rise above it to find success and happiness? How did you make lemonade out of the lemons life gave you?

My mother may never be able to see me as a unique individual separate from her own identity; she may never be able to love me for who I am, and while I still hope for that unconditional love from her, I can now see her through compassionate eyes. The mind of a narcissist is filled with fear. They have to be hypervigilant and in control of every situation they encounter. That's an impossible task, and it must be a torturous existence inside her mind. But I can no longer live in the hope that somehow, someday, she will change. I have to move on with my life. I have to let go of the past.

While this is something that happened to me, it is no longer "my story." I have a new story—one of healing and self-love. I have my mother figure secure inside of me. I have evicted the introjected mother figure I had for most of my life and replaced her with my own image of unconditional love; my inner mother is giving unconditional love to my inner child. She is helping that little me to heal. Even my mother sees the change in me, and of course, she doesn't like it. But that's okay because I do. Each person has their own story and their own life puzzle, and each of us has to complete the puzzle for ourselves. We can't do it for anyone else, and no one can do it for us. We must walk our own path. I continue on my path of healing, but what does your path look like? What is your story, and how did you get to this point?

Exercise #4

What's Your Type?

To assess your type of codependency, you'll need to consider your answers to the following questions carefully. Be honest, and remember—you're doing this to help yourself be free from your fears.

- When your intimate partner leaves for work or to go out with friends, do you feel anxious?
- Do you ever say something to a loved one in an effort to get them to respond to you in a particular way? For example, you might say something like, "I'm so stupid," to get them to disagree with you.
- Do you secretly wish that other people would recognize your efforts in supporting someone you love?
- Do you consider yourself independent?
- Have you ever feigned an illness to get a loved one to stay at home with you?
- Have you ever threatened suicide if a loved one leaves you?
- Do you like to think of yourself as a rebel?
- Do you see yourself as the star of a Greek tragedy?
- Do you think the reason your loved one is successful is because of your support?
- Do you ever feel like you push people away and then pull them close again?

Once you've answered these questions, reflect on your answers and determine which types of codependency they fit the best. There can be overlaps, as exemplified by my own story, but there is likely one that will fit better than the others. Remember, the goal is to understand the nature of your type of codependency fully. That knowledge will pave the way toward your personal healing path.

Chapter 5

Your Restless Inner Child

Do you remember when you were a child and the summers seemed endless? Do you remember being fascinated by the simple beauty of a butterfly? Do you remember the wonder of discovery when first learning about the world around you? What about just laying on a hillside and watching the clouds go by? The joy of playing with your friends, the laughter, and the freedom you felt as you just enjoyed life?

The peace, wonder, curiosity, playfulness, and joy of just being—those are the gifts a child possesses. A child is like a budding scientist exploring the world around them and taking in new knowledge and experiences. They observe, experiment, and learn. They are unencumbered by preconceived notions of what should and shouldn't be. They accept what is, and they adapt. But there's a dark side to that as well: when there is abuse, neglect, indifference, or perhaps even just distance in the family, children absorb those experiences, and it can affect them for the rest of their lives. We have learned that even before an infant is able to speak or walk, they are already absorbing the experiences from their environment and caretakers.

That inner child that's a part of each one of us remembers those experiences and holds onto anything traumatic. Specifically, they hold our memories, emotions, and beliefs from the past, and they also store our hopes and dreams for the future. They remember how grandma smelled when she hugged you and the look of pride on your mother or father's face when you mastered something. They remember what we desired to be when we grew up. They remember that feeling of awe and wonder you got when you envisioned doing what you loved so much.

Your inner child also, however, remembers what it felt like to be bullied at school. They remember how you felt when your teacher scoffed at your awkward answer to a seemingly easy question. They also remember if your mother or father didn't look at you as an infant with love; if instead, they looked at you with irritation or outright disdain. Basically, your inner child has been inside of you, storing away any memories, feelings, and thoughts you experienced when those events happened. Your inner child is like a vast storehouse of sensations, good and bad, that you've had every moment of your life. Even long after you've forgotten an incident, your inner child remembers the incident and your accompanying emotions. That little part of you is with you even today, waiting to be heard, understood, and loved. They are always communicating with you, but you may not know how to listen and respond.

That's the goal of focusing on your inner child—to see, acknowledge, and embrace them with the unconditional love they deserve. It's important to do that because your inner child can affect your life significantly. You might experience their influence when you're starting a new intimate relationship, and as soon as that person starts to get close to you, you are seized by an uncontrollable sense of fear. Your inner child is letting you know there's a problem that you need to address. They are crying out for attention because they remember an experience from your past. Ignoring them won't do because they can make or break your happiness. If you're feeling frustrated in some part of your life, that's likely your inner child trying to get your attention. Tending to them is one of the most important things you will do in your life.

The Origins of Inner Child Theory

Eric Berne first introduced the term "Inner Child" in the 60s. He associated it with the child ego state, which he described as having become enriched to become the "Inner Child." Later, researchers began exploring how a patient can reclaim their inner child to rediscover their deeper selves and heal old wounds. It became a way to nurture one's psychological well-being when examining trauma related to codependency. Inner child healing workshops became a way for traumatized individuals to do this work in a safe group setting. These workshops allow them to connect with their inner child, soothe their wounds, and then experience a rebirth into a new caretaking experience, where they would learn how to parent their inner child with love and support. Essentially, you would give them what they should have gotten from your caretakers, but that didn't happen. After all, we are all adult kids just trying to understand our world.

Studies consistently show that people of all ages can benefit from this type of intervention. It can help heal old wounds, and doing so can then work to help you become more childlike in beneficial ways. Healthy children have an undeniable capacity for finding the good in every situation, and they are infinitely creative. That's what I mean when I say healing your inner child will help you reclaim that childlike innocence beneficially. You become your own hero, and you save yourself from the inner demons that seek to undermine you. You can overcome old fears and anxieties that are making you feel stuck. When you heal those old wounds, you can see and change the unhelpful behavioral patterns that are preventing you from blossoming.

How Do You Connect to and Heal Your Inner Child?

There are two steps to cultivating a relationship with your inner child. You must first make that connection to begin a dialogue and develop a relationship with them. You have to see them and be willing to listen to them. After making that connection, the next step is to listen to what they're telling you. You have to learn about what scares them, hurts them, what they dream about, and what their hopes are. Once you know that, you can then provide your inner child with what they need to thrive. By giving them what they need, you are giving *yourself* what you need. What you do for your inner child, you do for yourself.

Connecting with Your Inner Child

To connect with your inner child, you have to connect with your core beliefs. One of the best ways to do that is through meditation. When you sit in silence with the emotions that have been triggered by an event, you can begin exploring what is actually causing your reaction. For example, one of the things that used to trigger me was criticism. Because of my mother's constant criticism, my inner child was hypersensitive to anything critical that anyone would say to me. When I began doing inner child work, I would call up a recent incident where I had been triggered by some kind of criticism. I would meditate on the incident so I could experience the feeling again. Afterwards, I would go a little deeper and explore the first time I felt that way. Inevitably, I would see a little girl being criticized in some similar way by her angry mother. I would see that little me shrinking in shame. When I was a child, I tried so hard to please my mother, but no matter what I did, she had some kind of criticism. It generated a core belief of shame and unworthiness in that little me. When I tapped into those emotions, I could see myself withering under her critical assessment of not just my actions that she had issues with, but of who I was. When I could see that little girl being crushed by the shame her mother was instilling in her, I was then able to comfort, tell her that there is nothing wrong with her, and assure her that I would always be here to take care of her. I could address that pain and help her heal that old wound.

Healing Your Inner Child

Just by shining a light on that trauma, we can achieve a lot of healing. When we listen to our inner child, we give ourselves a way to process that old pain. Often, the trauma that you receive at a young age gets "stuck" in your body. We were never able to process it, and for that reason, it stayed stuck. It is that trapped trauma that continues to affect our daily lives negatively. Your inner child needs to be heard and understood, and they need your attention. Sometimes they just need your support, but in other cases, they can also give you guidance. My little girl didn't have a voice all those years ago; she couldn't speak up to defend herself. When she sees that I'm in a similar situation as an adult, she gets distressed because she wants me to speak up not just for myself, but for her as well. She needs me to take care of myself and, thereby, take care of her. She is insistent on that, and to make her point, she is able to generate all kinds of uncomfortable feelings that would affect my relationships. Once I start doing that, once I start meeting her needs – which are also my needs – the uncomfortable feelings go away. Think about this in terms of your own relationships. What is your inner child saying to you, and when do they speak up?

When Your Inner Child is Happy

When your inner child is happy and healthy, it will fill you with energy and creativity. Gone are the latent feelings of shame and fear. Failure is something that happens to you occasionally; it is not who you are. You no longer need to act out impulsively, and you don't need approval from others. You can blossom into who you've always believed you were because you are anchored by a strong, healthy, internal "family." Gone are the insecurity and introjected negative mother figure. You replace her as a healthy parental figure for your inner child. You feel confident, rooted, secure, and comfortable in your own skin, and you can see the path that is right for you more clearly. Additionally, your inner child can act as a kind of guide. They are more open to you now that you're meeting their needs, and they can alert you to your deepest emotions and desires, while also helping you take better care of yourself. We often don't know when our subconscious is trying to tell us something, but when we're in communication with our inner child, we have a direct line to those fears and desires. This can help us uncover the hidden emotions we may have buried long ago. It's a deeply satisfying form of healing.

What are the Symptoms of a Restless Inner Child?

So how can you know if your inner child is trying to get your attention? What are the symptoms that suggest you need to do this kind of work? Here are some of the more common indications that your inner child likely needs your attention.

- Feelings of shame, guilt, and/or pain.

- You're a workaholic, and you feel you need to achieve or produce to get approval or to feel as though you belong.
- You are always thinking about the past or future. You are never in the present.
- You regularly feel anxious and fearful.
- You are rigid in your behavior and personality, and you believe you must be perfect. Failure on any level distresses you greatly.
- You have difficulty celebrating victories in life and accepting compliments. You readily accept criticism but feel that any compliment is just someone "being nice."
- You have a pattern of unhealthy relationships, or you avoid committed relationships altogether.
- You sabotage yourself in your relationships and career path. You often do this through addictive behaviors.
- You are an underachiever. You have great potential, but you just don't do the work.
- You have a negative internal critic. You ruminate on what you have said in conversations, sometimes for days after the conversation has taken place.

These are just a few of the signs that indicate your inner child is restless. For each of these, there is an underlying core belief that you've accepted about yourself.

What are Core Beliefs?

Core beliefs represent the essence of how we see ourselves, the world around us, and other people. They also involve what we think of our potential and what we might do in the future. They are "stored" by our inner child, since they form early in life. Certain situations can activate these core beliefs; for example, I couldn't believe that other people really thought I was attractive. When they would tell me so, I simply thought they were being nice or trying to make me feel better. Why was that? I had adopted a core belief that my mother had told me from an early age that I have nothing to offer anyone—I am ugly and worthless. Because my mother started telling me those things early in life, I simply accepted them. This is what children do, particularly when they're being told by an authority figure that something is true. These core beliefs are deeply rooted and inflexible. They cause you to readily accept any life situation that confirms your core belief and ignore evidence that contradicts it. I couldn't accept a compliment about my appearance, but I could readily accept that my relationships failed because I am inherently worthless.

To challenge these core beliefs, you have to comfort your inner child and show them that they are not true. That means you have to challenge the core beliefs head-on. For example, if you hold a core belief that you're stupid, and that belief is activated because you failed a test in school, you may initially accept that your failure proves that you are stupid. But when you examine it a little more closely and honestly, the truth is that you simply didn't study for the test. You might not have studied because you had to work or you had an emergency come up. You might also be engaging in a form of self-sabotage. All of these are possibilities, but none of them indicate stupidity. Moreover, it wasn't that you couldn't understand the material presented on the test; it was that you were ignorant of the right answer. Ignorance is not the same as stupidity. When you examine the situation objectively, you accumulate evidence to support how your core belief is not true. You can find other examples too, and as they become more apparent, they can be used to convince your inner child that this core belief is not valid. Uncovering your core beliefs is at the heart of inner child work. They represent what your inner child has come to believe, which is a big part of why they can stir up restlessness in your conscious life.

One of my core beliefs was that I was not enough. My mother had reinforced that belief on many occasions, but there's more to that belief than simply what her words told me. I also absorbed it in her face when she looked at me as an infant. She didn't mirror love and acceptance; she mirrored irritation and dissatisfaction. I introjected a message of not being enough for my mother. She loved my brother, and he could do no wrong—he was, after all, the golden child—but I was nothing but a source of disappointment for her from the day I was born until now. This is a strong core belief, and if I'm completely honest, I have yet to banish it forever. But the inner child work I have done has helped me greatly to recognize when that belief gets activated, as well as dealing with it healthier and more effectively. It's important to remember that all of this work is a process. Lifelong trauma is healed over time. The first step is connecting to your inner child and discovering your core beliefs.

Exercise #5

Connection and Discovery

This exercise is designed to help you get in touch with your inner child and discover your core beliefs, and it will provide a template for doing so. You'll need a quiet place for self-reflection and your journal. It can also help to play some meditative music while going through this process.

Connection

- Sit in a quiet place where you won't be disturbed.
- Close your eyes and focus on your breathing.
- Take ten deep breaths that expand your belly and chest.
- When you feel relaxed, call to mind something that happened recently that triggered you—a situation where you had an emotional reaction without fully understanding why.
- Relive the experience and fully feel the emotion it created.
- What emotion are you feeling? Is it shame, anger, pain, or fear? Name it and try to think of the first time you experienced that emotion.
- What is your first conscious memory of feeling that emotion? Who was there? What happened? What was said or done? Why did you feel that emotion?

What made you afraid? Who said something that made you feel ashamed? What did they say?
- Look at that little you in that situation. Can you see yourself? Do you see your frightened, ashamed, or angry little self? Can you go up to them and comfort them?
- What is the core belief behind the emotional reaction? What did that little child come to believe because of what someone said or did to them?
- Tell that little you that the core belief they adopted isn't true. Tell them you love them unconditionally and that you will always be there for them.
- Take ten more deep breaths, and when ready, open your eyes.

Reflection

After completing the meditative part of the exercise, write in your journal about what you experienced. Answer the following prompts:

- What was the situation that happened when you first felt that emotion?
- Describe it in detail.
- What did it make you feel?
- What was the core belief you adopted as a result of this interaction?

Write for as long as necessary. Try to get to the root of the belief. For example, you might have felt fear, but what's behind that fear? It may be that you felt afraid because you also felt helpless. The fear only represents one expression of the helplessness you were truly feeling. Then, what kind of core belief did that generate? Did feeling helpless make you adopt the belief that you are weak, inept, and incapable? Did it make you believe you are useless or worthless? As you can see, there may be more complex, underlying beliefs behind your experience. It's important to dig out all the nuances behind your beliefs to truly begin the healing process.

Chapter 6

Gifts from the Shadows

The trauma we experience in life lives on in our shadows, and in that sense, it follows us through life. It has a strong influence on our behavior, and we don't consciously understand why or how it is affecting us. This is what psychologist Carl Jung referred to as "the doorway to the real." It contains our darkest desires, secret shame, and most intense rage. It is formed from our repressed memories and qualities—the parts of us we shun. We learned that these parts of ourselves are unacceptable from our culture or parents. But we can't keep it buried. Like a bizarrely distorted Phoenix, it rises from the ashes of our distant past. It reaches out to force us to acknowledge its presence. And to truly heal from our trauma, we must not only acknowledge its presence, but we must also embrace that darkness. The first part of this process is understanding how the shadow forms and controls our behavior.

How Your Shadow Self Forms

When we're born, we are whole, pure, and untouched by the challenges life brings. That doesn't last long; however, soon after, our shadow is also born. It forms as a byproduct of the interactions we have with our closest family members. These are our caretakers who tend to point out the parts of us that aren't so good. Part of that process is simply our socialization into the culture to which we belong. But often, part of that process involves trauma resulting from unhealthy actions and beliefs of our caretakers. In either case, they teach us to reject those perceived negative parts of ourselves so we can behave appropriately, whether that means within the context of our culture or in our interactions with our family members. Naturally, we learn to repress those parts of ourselves to prevent others from seeing them. After all, we don't want others to see the parts of us that are selfish, aggressive, or shameful in any way. But the shadow doesn't go away. Rather, it rises from the depths of our psyche to radically shape our behavior.

How Does the Shadow Self Affect Our Behavior?

To answer this question, it can help to see a few examples of how the shadow forms and the subsequent effects it has on our lives. Well, look into a few of my clients and friends and see how their shadow selves affected you, even if the intentions behind their caregivers' behavior were good.

One client is an older woman whose mother would always admonish her as a child that "pretty is as pretty does." Her mother was trying to convey that real beauty means being beautiful on the inside. Now, that seems like a pretty good message to teach a child; they need to be more concerned about someone's character than their physical beauty. The client, however, discussed how she distorted this message in a way that a shadow self-formed. She took her mother's saying to heart, to the degree that when she had bad thoughts, she would conclude that she was not pretty on the inside. She was ugly, and that equated to bad. So when she got angry or was selfish or vain, that was proof that she was really ugly. As a result, she repressed her angry, selfish, vain self and would often undermine her best interests in favor of not appearing to be a bad person. She wouldn't express justified anger, for example, or do things that were a necessary part of self-care. It set her up for codependency, in that it often caused her to neglect her needs so she wouldn't appear selfish. Still, on the inside, she sometimes had selfish, angry, and vain thoughts, and thus, she was consumed by shame. This had a dramatic effect on her adult relationships: she became a people pleaser to prove that she was worthy of love and not a bad person.

Another example comes from a male client who was consistently told that he shouldn't cry because "big boys don't cry." This is a common message often passed down from father to son in the attempt to turn boys into men who are acceptably masculine culturally. So as a child, his sensitive side was successfully suppressed and a tough shadow self-formed. When he grew up, he struggled in his relationships because he could not express his emotions, either good or bad, for fear of appearing to be a "sissy." He was also overly aggressive, which brought an end to many of his adult relationships. He became fearful of allowing himself to be seen by his friends and closest family members. He expressed a strong sense of isolation, and as a result, he struggled with loneliness and depression.

What's even worse, the more you repress the shadow, the more it grows and strengthens its influence in your life. As you can see, in the two examples above, the caretakers weren't abusing their children with the messages they sent; they were trying to convey culturally appropriate messages to teach their children how to behave acceptably. They wanted to turn them into what they—and the broader culture—considered *good*. They weren't beating them or emotionally abusing them, but still, the shadow formed as the children interpreted the messages they were receiving. Then, their shadows began to have a strong subconscious effect on their life. Can you think of any examples of this kind of message distortion in your own life? It's not something you can normally see clearly. It often expresses itself as emotions or a ghost-like "sense of what is right." But a distortion of messages is not the only way a shadow can form. Sometimes, the messages are born out of trauma.

How Does Trauma Affect Shadow Formation?

Shadows can also form from different types of trauma, and according to Lise Bourbeau, there are five types of trauma that can interfere with your life:

- Rejection
- Abandonment
- Humiliation

- Betrayal
- Injustice

When exposed to one of these types of trauma, we form a mask as protection against further trauma. When we don that mask, we also repress the part of ourselves that we believe provoked the trauma, which would then become a shadow. I have personally experienced the trauma associated with rejection and abandonment, as well as humiliation. These traumas laid the groundwork for the formation of my codependency. To better understand, let's examine each of these traumas, how they form, and the effects they can have on your life.

1. Rejection

Rejection can happen as early as an infant gazing into the irritated, unaccepting eyes of a disapproving parent. Perhaps the child was unplanned and unwanted, or perhaps they were outright rejected by their caretaker, usually a same-sex caretaker. This effectively brands the child as irrelevant and unwelcome. As the child grows, they start to believe more strongly that they are not wanted, and they try to disappear. They often wear the mask of the "runaway." This can even manifest in their physical form. They may be thin to the point of being skinny. Because they view themselves as unwanted, they feel awkward in the company of others, don't talk much, strive to be perfect because they've already been branded as unwelcome, and are constantly trying to prove they are worthy of love. They seek solace in solitude to avoid the stress of needing to show their worth constantly. They often look for an escape from their own anxiety through the abuse of various substances in hopes that it will help them disappear, become someone else, and/or just stop the pain.

2. Abandonment

This trauma often occurs from some type of abandonment by the opposite-sex parent. They may not have actually left the home, but they may have been distant or neglectful, and thus have emotionally abandoned the child.

Another female client of mine suffered from this trauma due to the aloofness of her father in the first four years of her life. Her father was a narcissist, and he had little to do with her early on. He didn't even visit her in the hospital as an infant. He abandoned her emotionally, and although her mother was a loving presence in her life, his abandonment resulted in numerous problems in her adult relationships. She became clingy to satisfy her hunger for her father's love, which he never gave her. She needed to have someone need her love and fell into codependency as a result. Her romantic partners, however, were subconsciously chosen for their similarities to her father, and to avoid having them abandon her, she often left them before they could leave her. It was a way to strike back at her father; however, it was never fulfilling, given that it wasn't actually her father. She always felt a void inside that she could never seem to fill until she was able to resolve the abandonment trauma she had suffered. Other manifestations of abandonment trauma include emotional dysregulation—laughing one minute and crying the next—dramatization, fear of loneliness, and depression. Physical displays include migraine headaches and asthma, among others.

3. Humiliation

This type of trauma results from an overly critical parenting style. It is particularly devastating for a child to hear criticism from their mother at a young age, although this type of wound can still occur at any age. This is a trauma with which I am very familiar. The humiliated child dons the mask of the masochist, which means they subconsciously look for problems and develop a low sense of self-worth from constant criticism and repeated humiliation. This, too, can result in codependency, as the sufferer strives to help others but then, voluntarily and subconsciously, becomes part of the problem, given that they are motivated out of fear and shame. This person is hypersensitive to criticism but often offends others without realizing it. Physical manifestations include back problems and respiratory diseases, out of feeling suffocated by the weight of their burden. Likewise, these individuals neglect their own needs in favor of helping others.

4. Betrayal

Betrayal is usually experienced when we are between the ages of two to four years old, and it is often the opposite-sex parent who perpetrates this trauma. This was another trauma suffered by my client, "Marie," whom I mentioned in the abandonment section. Her father often betrayed her trust by not keeping his word, seeming to prefer other people and emotionally abusing her. This type of trauma can cause an individual to become very controlling, which was true of Marie as well. She felt responsible for everything in her world and would strive to control herself, other people, and the circumstances in a given environment. She was extremely demanding of herself and others and was often disappointed when she or others failed to live up to her high standards. She would suffer an emotional breakdown when situations spiraled out of her control, and to prevent that from happening, she would not only come up with a Plan B, but also a Plan C, D, E, F, etc. Physical manifestations of betrayal trauma often come in the form of joint problems and digestive system issues. Marie had painful problems with her knees.

5. Injustice

This type of trauma usually occurs with the same-sex parent between the ages of three and five years old. This child has suffered a trauma that they have deemed unfair. A friend of mine suffered from this kind of trauma when her stepbrothers were taken from her family by their biological mother when she was just five years old. They had lived as one big happy family for two years, and suddenly, they were gone. It was all done due to the actions of adults without any consideration for the children. She experienced an injustice and, as a result, she put on a protective mask. She became rigidly perfectionist and was extraordinarily frustrated by those things she perceived were acting unfairly. For her, it was like she was experiencing her trauma all over again. Like anyone who suffers this kind of trauma, she was extremely hardworking, to the point of being a workaholic. But she would often exhaust herself to the point of a nervous breakdown. She lived in almost constant fear of making a mistake and disappointing other people. This would frequently cause her to lose sleep, which would become a major problem for her.

The 5 Traumas and Shadow Formation

As you might imagine, there are several opportunities for shadow formation when subjected to these kinds of trauma. An angry shadow may form, for example, with any of these traumas. The angry shadow tries to protect you from not only further trauma, but also your actions born as a result of the original trauma. For example, the client who suffered from abandonment trauma became codependent to fill a need for love. She related that she often felt "put upon" by her romantic partners who, being similar to her father, took advantage of her codependency. Although her shadow self harbored extreme resentment and anger toward these men, she feared expressing that anger because she didn't want them to leave her. That caused her to feel ashamed as well as angry at herself for being a "doormat." She couldn't express that anger, however, because anger was not socially acceptable and might endanger her relationship. Her angry self was her shadow self. It was a part of herself that she denied and hid from others and from herself.

My own rejection and humiliation from my mother resulted in low self-worth. I believed I was worthless and became a people-pleaser in an attempt to love myself. My mother's criticism made me fearful of making mistakes, and I became perfectionist as a result. I hid and rejected my lazy, bumbling shadow self because I saw it as imperfect and undesirable.

Likewise, people who experience the trauma of injustice hide their unfair shadow self from the world. They deny its existence because they know the pain of injustice and don't want to think they could ever treat others unfairly. This is one way we can recognize our shadow self. If there is someone who says or does something that bothers you, that's an indicator that your shadow self is seeking recognition. Can you think of how some of your pet peeves might indicate a hidden shadow? Maybe you feel overly bothered by someone who appears inefficient. That might indicate a lazy or inefficient shadow self. Perhaps it bothers you when someone wears something you consider inappropriate. You feel irritated by it to where you might even choose to say something about it. This could be because you are denying your "ugly" shadow self forged from an old rejection trauma you suffered. Your shadow self is something you don't want to believe is true about yourself. It's something you see as weak or unacceptable, and you can't accept it as a part of yourself. But every shadow brings a gift that can help us deal with those old traumas.

What is the Gift of the Shadow?

We deny their existence and bury them deep within our psyche because they often form as a result of trauma. But the shadow self is often the key to healing that trauma. In fact, it is only by accepting our shadow and acknowledging the gifts it brings that we can fully heal from those old wounds. How can you recognize the gifts of her shadow self? Let's look at a few examples.

- **Anger**—We are often taught by our families and society at large that anger is dangerous and should not be expressed. We reject it out of fear that it will cause us to be rejected or abandoned, humiliated or betrayed, or treated unfairly. But anger won't be denied, and as long as you express it healthily, it can help you set appropriate boundaries.
- **Imperfection**—Many of the traumas above can cause fear of imperfection. We don't want to be seen as flawed because we could be rejected, abandoned, or humiliated. But our imperfections help us cultivate self-compassion and self-forgiveness. When we can have compassion and forgiveness for ourselves, we can also express those sentiments for others.
- **Vulnerability**—Vulnerability is seen culturally and individually as a bad quality, one you don't want to possess. No one wants to be seen as vulnerable or weak. We push our perceived weaknesses deep inside. But being vulnerable opens us up to intimacy with others. Without the ability to be vulnerable and expose your weaknesses, it becomes very difficult to get close to another person.

So our shadow selves have valuable gifts to share with us, but to receive those gifts, we must first accept our shadow. To do that, we must heal the traumas that created them in the first place.

Exercise #6

You and Your Shadow

In this exercise, the goal is to help you identify the types of trauma you may have suffered in your own childhood, as well as the shadow selves you might have created as a result. Let's first look at the type of trauma you may have suffered.

Which Mask Do You Wear?

Circle the number that represents your experience the closest for each statement or question:

Which body type best describes your body?

- Skinny.
- Slender or normal, but lacking muscle tone.
- Plump or obese with a round face
- Strong body—in men, shoulders are wider than the lower body, and in women, the lower body is wider (pear-shaped).
- Well-proportioned but small and rigid.

Which of the following characterizes your behavior?

- You seek solitude and don't get attached to material things.
- You always need help and support, and your emotions are a roller coaster.

- You are messy, don't feel attractive, and reward yourself with food.
- You are uncompromising, interrupt others frequently, and are angered by inefficiency and laziness.
- You are a perfectionist but often doubt your choices; you can be short-tempered and have problems showing affection.

Which description best characterizes your relationships?

- You prefer solitude and don't speak up much in a group.
- You seek approval from others and have difficulty making decisions without their support.
- You do everything for others but blame yourself for everything as well, and even take the blame for other people.
- You have difficulty delegating tasks; you make backup plans for everything.
- You don't like to show your emotions, but you act to ensure others believe you deserve a reward.

Which of the following is true for you?

- You often use words like null, nothing, or disappear.
- You often use phrases like "I can't stand," "I'm being eaten…," or "I give up."
- You often use words like dignified, fat, dirty, unworthy, or pig.

- You often use phrases like "Let me do it," "Trust me," or "Do you understand."
- You often use words or phrases like "no problem," "always," "never," or "very good."

Which of the following would you say is your biggest fear?

- Panic
- Loneliness
- Freedom
- Disengagement, separation, dissociation, or denial
- Coldness

Once you have finished answering the questions, tally up your score. While there can be overlap, scores indicate the following:

- 5 - 8: Runaway mask associated with a wound of rejection.
- 9 - 12: Addict mask associated with a wound of abandonment.
- 13 - 17: Masochist mask associated with a wound of humiliation.
- 18 - 21: The Controller mask associated with a wound of betrayal.
- 22 - 25: The Rigid mask associated with a wound of injustice.

Although this is not a perfect system for identification of trauma, because you can suffer more than one trauma type, it should still give you a general idea of where you fall on the trauma scale. Once you have identified a type or types of trauma, reflect on its origins in a journal. This can help you further uncover old memories associated with traumatic events. Explore this old trauma as you feel is helpful for understanding your current behavior.

The Shadow Knows

The key to recognizing your shadow self lies in identifying what irks you the most. The things that trigger you often do so because you subconsciously believe them to be a part of yourself, and you have rejected that part. To find your shadow, you must delve into the depths of your psyche and explore what bothers you and why. Reflect on something that triggered you recently—something small that wasn't even associated with someone you know. Maybe you saw someone doing something and got very angry, or someone said something that you perceived negatively, and you judged that person harshly. Relive that experience in your mind as you reflect on the following prompts:

- What happened that bothered you?
- What did you perceive about the situation that made you judge those involved?
- What judgment did you make?
- What are your feelings about that—for example, if you judged them to be vain, why do you think vanity is so wrong, and can there be anything good about it?
- Can you remember the first time you felt judgmental about such a behavior or situation?
- Have you ever been judged in that way?

- Do you think you possess any level of that quality or trait?
- What would it mean if you did?

Write in as much detail as you can when responding to the prompts, but feel free to continue exploring your thoughts and emotions about this subject. Discovering the shadow and the trauma behind it is an important step toward healing.

Chapter 7

From Denial to Acceptance

Sometimes, it's very difficult to accept that you are codependent. After all, no one wants to admit that they are a people pleaser. Many times, they equate it with weakness, but that's not really what's going on. Codependency has little to do with your strength of character. It's all about the conditioning you received, both consciously and subconsciously, as a child. Still, the common perception is that you're somehow weak and obsequious. One client of mine, whom I'll call "Kate," gives a perfect example of this. She had suffered the traumas of rejection and abandonment by her father when she was young. Additionally, her codependent mother had modeled people-pleasing behaviors throughout her life. Moreover, her mother had tried to train her in codependency by telling her that it was her responsibility to take care of her disabled brother and younger sister. She was saddled with responsibility at a very young age, and as an adult, she saw herself as an independent, strong, and confident woman. She did indeed possess those qualities, but she had a history of failed relationships, and in each, she had been the one to leave. Her pattern was one of becoming involved with a man who was aloof and distant in some way, similar to her father. She would do many things for that man, but she would also push him to prove his love. Then, before he could leave, she would end the relationship. Her partners were often surprised by the way she ended things.

Finally, Kate met a man whom she actually married. By that time, she had realized her pattern of choosing men similar to her father and trying to relive that relationship with better results. But she thought she had finally broken the pattern. Unfortunately, although the man she married was very expressive of his love for her, he was also narcissistic just like her father. Over the course of their marriage, she had given in to his desires for things he wanted to do or have on many occasions, and this was despite the fact that she didn't want those things and didn't want to do what he did. Still, she saw that as evidence that she was a reasonable spouse who wasn't trying to control her husband. She wasn't a nag; she was an open, enlightened spouse. Because of her husband's choices and her support of those choices, the couple fell into financial problems. She was once again saddled with the lion's share of responsibility for supporting the family, this time financially. One day, her husband told her he had won a dinner with two nights and three days at a hotel. My client realized this was likely a sales tactic, and that when they went to the dinner, someone would try to sell them a timeshare or some other service. She mentioned this to her husband and told him that they were not going to buy anything they pitched, no matter how good it sounded.

Kate was correct about the sales pitch, but despite what she had said, her husband very much wanted to buy what they were selling. This time, however, she stood firm. She told him that she didn't know where they would come up with the extra money to pay for what this company was selling; since it would be her responsibility to pay, the answer was no. He grudgingly agreed and told them no sale. As they were going home, however, my client couldn't shake feeling upset that she had been unable to give her husband what he wanted. She felt like she had disappointed him. She explained that she experienced a sudden insight about herself that she had previously been denying—she was, in fact, codependent, and moreover, it was the result of long-term conditioning from her father's rejection and abandonment, in addition to her mother's training. She could suddenly see how she had introjected that sense that she was responsible for providing other people with what they wanted and needed, even if that came at her own expense. It was that insight and acceptance that was key to setting her free. Once she could see her own codependency and how it affected her behavior, she could take steps toward finally healing.

Acceptance is one of the most difficult things you'll ever do. But without acceptance, there can be no healing. You can't heal something that you don't accept as a reality. You have to see clearly and honestly what is going on to deal with it effectively. Acceptance is the final step in the stages of grief identified by a Swiss American psychiatrist, Elisabeth Kübler-Ross. The key to dealing with grief effectively, she determined, was by finally arriving at the stage of acceptance. Though she worked specifically on grief, we go through these same stages when dealing with any change or unexpected event. When working on your personal growth, you go through significant change and work through those changes by navigating the stages of grief. In a way, you are grieving. You're grieving the loss of the old, so you may celebrate the arrival of the new. Even if what you are leaving behind is something that no longer serves you, you go through a form of grief when transitioning to a new life. But how exactly do we go from denial to acceptance and heal codependency?

Moving Past Denial

The key to getting to acceptance is moving past denial. That's the first step in those five stages outlined by Kübler-Ross. From there, you would pass through the other stages of anger, bargaining, and depression before arriving at acceptance. When Kate reflected on her process of acceptance, she reflected on how she had passed through the other stages. She had initially denied her codependency, but after having her insights that fateful evening, she became very angry. She was angry at her mother and father for having saddled her with this condition. But more than that, she was angry with herself for allowing other people to take advantage of her for that long. It took some honest shadow work for her to embrace her people-pleasing shadow. She was able to do that when she embraced the gifts that that side of herself brought. After all, that part of her had good intentions. It wanted to help others and was just trying to help her love herself. Her shadow self was trying to help her find a way to cherish the kind, supportive person she truly was. Once she saw the gifts from the shadow, she was able to move past her anger.

From there, she moved on to bargaining with her people-pleasing tendencies. Perhaps there was a compromise she could make to please everyone, including herself. It didn't take long for Kate to see that wasn't going to work. There was no being just a little bit codependent. She had to prioritize her needs and desires and see that she was worthy of being prioritized. But that brought on the depression associated with feeling like she was losing herself somewhere along the way. She expressed not really knowing who she had been all those years and who she was becoming now. But when she finally accepted what happened to her, she was able to move on from her codependent behavior. She could finally free herself of the burden of having to make everyone happy. She realized that she wasn't responsible for saving anyone other than herself. She wasn't responsible for anyone else's happiness, nor for providing for them either. She found that her life became much better all around as a result of these changes. Because she respected herself, the people around her also began to see her in a new light. They began to respect her, even though she wasn't giving them everything they wanted anymore. That made it much easier for her to cultivate her self-worth. This is the value of this healing strategy, and it exemplifies the importance of acceptance.

Seeing the Patterns

One of the most important facets of moving from denial to acceptance is taking an honest look at your behavioral patterns through the years. Usually, this is prompted by something that has happened. It's something that causes you to finally realize that something's got to give. If you're not in some level of pain, it's unlikely that you'll begin to move through the cycle of acceptance. Let's take a look at this cycle and how you might experience it.

Normal Life

Initially, you're going through your normal life. You're functioning well enough, and although you have some inner turmoil, it's not painful enough to prompt real change. For Kate, she had settled into her married life, and though she felt some level of discontent, it wasn't enough to cause any real movement.

The Pain Becomes Unbearable

The next stage in the cycle is that of the pain increasing to an unbearable level for some reason. In Kate's case, this happened when her mother passed away and left her with the responsibility of caring for her sister. Her sister had a personality disorder that her mother had enabled for the majority of her life. Her sister's learned helplessness was such that it was incapacitating. Her mother had left her with that huge responsibility. It was bad news that significantly increased the pain of her inner turmoil.

Then Comes Denial

Kate had long been in denial of her codependency, but she had also denied that her mother had been somehow at fault for the situation. She couldn't believe it was true; she didn't *want* to believe it was true. But the closer she looked, the more her denial crumbled away.

The Anger Stage

The next step in the process is anger. Kate was incredibly angry at her situation. She was angry at her sister and mother for putting her in this situation. Although she raged to herself privately, she didn't express this anger to those who were deserving of it. She even had trouble admitting her anger toward her mother, since she was now deceased. But she finally let herself feel that anger and expressed it. That was a breakthrough that led to the next stage.

Depression is Up Next

Initially, Kate was depressed because she felt overwhelmed and trapped. She didn't see any way out of the situation her mother had put her in. She didn't want to let her sister become homeless or have to be committed any more than her mother had wanted. Initially, all she could see was that she would have to take on this enormous, unfair responsibility.

Bargaining for a Solution

After that, Kate began to bargain for an acceptable solution. She had several ideas of what she might do that would take care of her sister's needs without her actually having to live with her. They all involved her taking on burdens that were not hers to bear. And they all required her continuing codependency.

Acceptance at Last

Finally, Kate arrived at the stage of acceptance. She accepted the problem for what it was, and she accepted both her mother's and her own role in creating it. That led to her realizing that she was, in fact, codependent. And when she finally could see that truth about herself, she could then take the steps she needed to heal. This is true for all of us. We see the world through the lens of our trauma, and to resolve those old wounds, we often unconsciously create repetitive scenarios in our lives that approximate the wounding relationship. It becomes like the metaphor in Don Quixote of fighting the windmills; it's an endless cycle such that it seems there is no way out. In reality, our traumas create illusions that obscure our vision. To see clearly, we have to accept the situation we are in and the reasons behind it. When that happens, it'll be as if we have finally removed the blinders preventing us from seeing clearly. We can then realize the mask we have donned and why. That's the first step toward healing.

So, what patterns have you seen in your own life? Do you have a history of troubled relationships? Does it feel overwhelming with certain responsibilities? What is your role in creating or perpetuating that situation? When you look back at cycles that involve the grief process, it can help you to identify those patterns. It's also helpful if you can explore your normal reactions to the grief cycle. For example, when you become angry, how do you typically express that anger? Do you fly off the handle or hold your anger inside? Maybe you even turn it inward toward yourself to avoid taking it out on someone else. This is a common pattern for codependents. In some ways, they work as hard at image control as toxic people do. They don't want people to see their anger or dissatisfaction, so they bury it and try to deal with those difficult emotions without appearing too expressive. In that way, they can continue to please the people in their life.

This was the battle that I fought in my own life. My mother was very critical, and I tried so hard to please her so she would love me, which would then give me permission to love myself. This is the struggle of the codependent—it's really what you're looking for, the sense of self-worth you need to love yourself. The problem is that you're delegating that power to someone else. You're looking for love in all the wrong places, as the song goes. Self-love cannot be found through anyone else, but the wounded self-esteem of the codependent can't see that. In one sense, they can't even see themselves anymore. Their whole life is geared toward pleasing other people; it feels as though they don't matter. It is through service to others that they find their self-worth, but self-worth must grow from within to be a healthy part of your identity. It's not something external that you can acquire; it's something you cultivate from self-love.

Exercise #7

What are Your Patterns?

As with the other exercises we've done, there are two parts to this exercise. The first is identifying your patterns, and the second is identifying your pain. Let's start with the patterns.

Lifelong Patterns

Begin by answering the prompts below, and then reflect on the patterns you see and what created them. What is the reason you do what you do? What makes you like certain things? What triggers you into making the choices you make?

- What kind of characteristics do you find attractive in a potential mate?
- How many intimate relationships have you had in your life?
- How long do your relationships typically last?
- Are you the one who ends those relationships, or does someone else?
- When you're in a relationship, do you normally make the rules in the household, or do you follow someone else's rules?
- How do you feel when you tell someone no?
- Do you work outside of the home? If so, what kind of work do you do?
- Do you prefer to be the boss or the employee?
- How do you feel if you can't do something someone has asked you to do?
- Do you worry that people won't like you if you don't do what they want?

After you've answered these questions, explore your answers a little more by noting the patterns you see and what they might mean to you. Can you identify specific reasons behind your behaviors? For example, if you have had several intimate relationships, but they don't last very long, can you identify a reason why? Are you afraid of getting too close? Do you sabotage those relationships? Write as much or as little as you need to in order to better understand your patterns of behavior. You're taking the blinders off to see clearer. To do that, you need to understand yourself better.

What Brought You Here?

The next step in this exercise is to explore your pain. You've arrived at reading this book for a reason. Something has prompted you to explore the roots of your behavior. What happened? Why did you take this significant step? Did you suffer the loss of a loved one, as Kate did? Did you break up with someone for the umpteenth time? Are you starting to think, "Maybe it's me?" What was the event or realization that prompted you to look for answers? I know I say it a lot, but write about it. When you write, you may gain insights you may not otherwise have. Let yourself explore where your writing goes; it may show you the way. From this point, we can start to explore what happens next.

Chapter 8

So You're Codependent—What Now?

When I realized my codependency, I knew I was going to have to face some very difficult emotions. I knew I would need the courage to dive into my past and explore my trauma. I knew this wasn't going to be easy, and it wasn't going to be a quick fix, but the hardest part was over. I had accepted my codependency, and that's when the healing began. There are a number of healing strategies you can employ for codependency. I'll discuss specific strategies in my next book on this subject, *Healing Codependency: How to Resolve Your Childhood Trauma so You Can Start Living Your Best Life,* but now you have some tools you can use for better insight into the problem. Let's explore a few more ideas to get you started.

Make a List and Check It Twice

The first step after realizing you're codependent is identifying your codependent behaviors. Once you've done that, you can determine the behaviors you want to achieve. Remember—you can't fix anything until you know what's wrong. My codependent behaviors consisted of subconsciously choosing partners similar to my mother so that I could "fix" the damaged relationship we had when I was a child. Now, you might think that I could just go talk to my mother and fix it that way. But the fundamental problem with trying to fix anything that happened in the past is that it already happened. Even if you can express your anger and pain to the person who wounded you, you can't undo the wound that way. Even if they acknowledge that they acted harshly or cruelly, that doesn't undo the harm they did. You've already incorporated that wound into your identity. That's also the problem with trying to fix a damaged relationship from your past through finding a similar partner. Even if I had chosen someone like my mother and convinced them to change, I would still have a wounded inner child who needed my attention.

Another behavior of mine that I identified was that I was always taking responsibility for the well-being of other people. Like Kate, I thought it was my responsibility to make other people happy. This is an attempt to love myself by pouring my love into someone else. When they return my love, it's as if I am giving myself love. But it's not the same, and it never will be. In fact, you can't really love someone else the way they deserve until you can love yourself. Moreover, it can cause a lack of boundaries. By taking on the responsibility of making someone else happy, I have to know their most private thoughts and desires. I have to be receiving feedback constantly. If they express any level of discomfort, I must act immediately to assuage the problem. It's an impossible task, and it's not my job. It also requires that I violate their boundaries and don't establish any of my own. I have never had boundaries because it's not something my mother would allow. I never learned what boundaries were until I began my own healing process. Now I can see how my codependency prevented healthy boundary formation, and it also prevented me from respecting other people's boundaries.

By taking on the responsibility for someone else's well-being and happiness, I was also creating another codependent behavior: an overreliance on someone else meeting my needs. I was looking to love myself, and to do that, I needed them to love me. In that way, I was relying on *them* to satisfy *my* need for something that only *I* could provide for myself. It's a situation that will never feel satisfying. I, like most codependents, feel a constant void inside—a yawning, empty hole that only genuine self-love can ever fill. Thus, no matter what I did or how much my partner seemed to love me, I never felt satisfied. I never felt like I was enough. Moreover, because I was so reliant on their feedback, I became hypervigilant of any changes in communication. If they seemed quiet, I interpreted that as them having stopped loving me. If they were angry, it must've been at me. If they were sad, I needed to entertain them. It was quite simply exhausting, and my self-esteem suffered because I could never get it right, just as I had never gotten it right in my mother's eyes. Here are some other codependent behaviors.

- Caretaking to the point of neglecting your own needs.
- Reacting emotionally rather than rationally.
- Feeling like you lost yourself.

- Feeling like you need to do whatever it takes to make someone else happy.
- A persistent feeling of emptiness that drives your service.

What are your characteristics of codependency? Think carefully about your behavioral patterns and write down the ones that might indicate codependency.

What Do You Want to Achieve?

The next part of identifying your codependent patterns is thinking carefully about what exactly you hope to achieve by doing this work. Something brought you here to learn more about codependency. What was the breaking point for you? What was the pain that became so great that you just had to act? And how do you hope learning about this behavioral pattern will alleviate the pain? Remember that for Kate, the breaking point was the death of her mother and the looming responsibility of caring for her sister. For me, it was yet another failed relationship. Similar to an alcoholic, codependents will often hit "rock bottom." That is the point at which the pain becomes so great that they can no longer ignore it. Essentially, you are forced to act, and although you might not think that learning more about the problem is acting, it's the first and most significant step in the journey toward healing. But to understand what to do next, you have to identify your goals. For most codependents, the ultimate goal is learning to love oneself and understanding their inherent value as distinct from anything they do in life. I am not valued based on my ability to maintain a relationship. Kate is not valued based on her ability to care for her sister. You are not valued based on your ability to please anyone other than yourself.

How do you achieve that sense of self-worth? It starts with identifying your behavioral patterns and then your goals for healing. For Kate, she wanted to be free of her self-worth being measured by how successful she could be at taking care of her sister and pleasing her mother. That's a heavy burden. For me, my goal was learning to love myself so I could love someone else for who they were. When you free yourself of that emptiness and replace that void with knowing you can be loved and supported no matter what, only then can you love someone else. You can genuinely want the best for them, even if that means they are not with you. Codependency is the opposite of that. They have to be with you because that's where you derive your self-love. If they leave, you will be abandoned yet again. In other words, you try to force them to be happy so you will feel happy and satisfied, but of course, that can't work. True happiness is grown from within. You have to break that habit of looking for an external source of self-worth and self-love. When you can do that, you can break free of the resulting behaviors tied to your search for fulfillment.

Breaking the patterns means first recognizing them, then replacing them with healthier habits. So let's look at a few ways you break out of the rigid patterns that guided your life to date.

❖ Change the View

As a codependent, you're accustomed to thinking of other people before yourself. To heal, you have to start changing your focus. Destructive self-neglect is one of the hallmarks of codependency, so you need to identify the needs you have been neglecting in favor of serving others.

This means looking inward and identifying exactly what you need. I needed time alone and therapy to process my patterns and break them. Kate needed distance from her overly attached mother and father. What do you need? Write it down.

❖ Find Yourself

When I began identifying what I needed, I was genuinely frightened about talking to my mother or anyone else about what I wanted for myself. I was so used to saying something like, "I'm good with whatever you decide," that I rarely ever voiced my opinion, even for something as simple as stating what I wanted to eat for dinner.

Codependents often fear voicing their desires because they are afraid they might upset someone around them. They don't want to be seen as selfish, but it's not selfish to state your preferences. You can practice this by starting with simple things. I began by saying, "I want Italian food tonight."

It seems like such a small step, but as Lao Tzu said, "A journey of a thousand miles begins with a single step." That first small step will lead you to the second, and the third, until you arrive at your goal. Identify a first step toward refocusing on yourself.

❖ Identify Your Limits

The next step is to identify your boundaries. This doesn't mean identifying what you won't do to please someone. It means identifying the boundaries you have for respecting yourself.

Boundaries are not about trying to get someone else to respect you; they are about respecting yourself. To identify my boundaries, I would think about times when I was hurt by someone, either by something they said or did. As I thought about those incidents, I could think about what made me feel disrespected by their actions.

For example, when my mother criticized me unfairly, I felt unloved. I also felt undervalued. Love and value were what I believed she was not giving me. She was crossing a line in failing to do so because she was my mother.

Another example comes from a friend of mine whose husband has a tendency to minimize her work. He constantly interrupts her workday to ask her to do something for him, and she's codependent too. What he was failing to respect was her contribution to the family's financial support. He was crossing a boundary.

Once you recognize your boundaries, you can protect them. For example, my friend would simply say to her husband, "I'm sorry. I can't do that right now. When I finish work, I can try to help." That was one small step toward respecting her contribution enough to say no.

I'll talk much more about how to identify, set, and protect your boundaries in my next book. For now, just try to identify boundaries and what you believe is lacking when someone violates them.

It Takes Time and Commitment

You've taken the first, and in some ways, the most important steps toward identifying your codependency patterns. You've accepted your codependency, and now, it's time to take action toward healing those old wounds and move into a better future. As you go down this road, it's important to remember that it takes time and commitment. You have to stick to your priorities of self-care, self-reflection, and processing the toxicity from external sources. This is the only way to heal. There are times when you may feel depressed; it's one of those grief stages we discussed before. But if you take the time to sit with your feelings and understand them, you will also begin to notice that those feelings shift; they are not forever. You will move from depression to the next stages until you reach acceptance. A common feature of the codependent personality is perfectionism. Codependents believe they have to get everything just perfect, or it's a reflection of what a failure they are, but you have to let that go. There is no such thing as perfect. Everything and everyone is a work in progress.

An important part of staying committed to your healing journey is self-awareness. This means you have to focus on your own feelings to understand how they are affecting your behavior. You need to process the times when you don't feel right about something. People often don't want to look at the reasons behind their behavior or feelings because they fear it will reveal something inherently bad about themselves. Nothing could be further from the truth. You are not inherently bad; you've just been conditioned to perform a certain way. Now, it's time to undo that conditioning because it's no longer serving you. When I was a confused, helpless child, my codependency was a survival mechanism. It got me through those difficult times. But now, I don't need it anymore. In fact, I know now that I need to prioritize my own needs and desires. That's where you are. Your codependency doesn't serve you anymore. It's time for new habits and a new path—a path toward healing old wounds and moving on to the life you want. You're a courageous person for undertaking such a journey, but you're not alone. Together, we can strive for a happier, healthier tomorrow.

Exercise #8

Mindfulness Meditation for Self-Awareness

One of the most important things you can do at this stage is to cultivate mindfulness and build self-awareness. You've been doing several exercises related to reflecting on your situation of codependency, and it's important to stay mindful while you do those. You may experience several emotions as you go through this process, and to advance your healing, you'll need to be aware of the changes you're going through, so you can process your feelings and make the best decisions on how to proceed. Meditation is one of the best techniques you can use for that purpose. It's important to cultivate a relationship with your body, thoughts, and feelings. After all, you've been denying your needs for so long that it's a strong habit to overcome. By re-engaging your awareness with your body and emotional changes, you can be aware of your needs in the present moment, so you can address them when they arise. This meditation exercise will help you to make that long journey from your mind to your heart.

To begin, you want to arrange for a place that is quiet and where you can be comfortable and undisturbed. It's helpful to make it into a real place of your own. You might place scented candles, comfortable seating, and appropriate lighting in this area. You'll also want to let anyone in your life know that when you're in this location, you are not to be disturbed. When you have this set up, it's a good idea to make a regular schedule for practicing your meditation. You don't have to meditate for a long time; even just a few minutes each day can help you make that connection between mind and body. You'll also want to have your journal stored in this location so you can write about any insights you experience. Once you're ready to meditate, set up the room accordingly, get seated comfortably, and allow yourself to relax. One final note before we begin—you don't have to sit cross-legged or in a lotus position for this to work. You can sit or even lie down, but you want to be in a position where you can remain alert. You don't want to fall asleep during this exercise. Now that you're comfortable and set up, let's move this guided meditation. If you would prefer, you can also record your voice, or someone else's soothing voice reading through this guided meditation, and then, you can play it back while meditating.

1. Get comfortable and close your eyes.
2. Take 10 deep breaths that expand both your stomach and your chest. Breathe in through your nose and out through your mouth.
3. Bring your attention to your breath and follow it as it enters through your nostrils, passes down the back of your throat, and expands your lungs. Count to four as you inhale.
4. Once your lungs are expanded, hold that breath and count to four again.
5. Exhale slowly to a count of eight. Follow your breath as it empties from your lungs, passes through your throat and into your mouth, and exits from your body.
6. Now, bring your focus to the top of your head. Notice any sensations you feel there. Does something itch? Does something tickle? Does something hurt? Can you feel a hat or anything else you have on your head?
7. If there is an area of pain, breathe deeply into that spot.
8. Move down your body to the back of your head, face, and neck. Notice any areas of pain, itchiness, or tickling. Breathe into anything that is uncomfortable.
9. From there, move down to your arms. Can you feel your hands resting on your lap or on the floor? Can

you feel the cloth of the shirt you have on? Do you feel any areas of pain or discomfort? Breathe into any such areas.

10. If your mind wanders during this process, just notice it and where it goes. Did you think about what you might make for dinner? That's planning. Did you worry about your bills? That's worrying. Whatever kind of thought you have when your mind wanders, label it as to the type, and then envision it wafting above your head and dissipating into the air, in the same way smoke rises from a campfire and dissipates into the sky above. Then gently and without judgment bring your focus back to your body.

11. Continue to move down into each area of your body—your chest, abdomen, pelvic region, legs, and feet. As before, notice any areas of discomfort and breathe into those areas. Be aware of the sensations you experience as you go through this process. Notice any change in your emotions and any thoughts you have.

12. Once you have moved through your entire body, bring your awareness back to your breath.

13. Take 10 more deep, belly and chest-expanding breaths, inhaling through the nose to a count of four, holding your breath for a count of four, and then exhaling through your mouth to a count of eight.

14. Thank your body for all it does for you, and thank yourself for taking care of your needs.

15. When you're ready, open your eyes.

Do this meditation several times, focusing solely on your body. Reflect in your journal about the sensations you experienced and the many ways in which your body tried to distract you from your mindfulness practice. You'll find you suddenly have an itch, for example, and it might even feel intense while you're meditating. This is your body's way of distracting you. Try not to move or scratch that itch; just notice how the sensation changes. The more you can sit with the sensations, the more your body will calm down during this practice. As we move on to healing, you'll use this meditation as a good springboard for exploring your deeper feelings and old wounding experiences that caused your codependence. For now, just become accustomed to the practice and make it a habit. You'll soon find that you can bring yourself into the present moment, even when you're not meditating. This will help you stay calm and think carefully about how to respond to stressful situations. It's a useful practice for managing stress as you go down the road to a solution.

Chapter 9

The Road to a Solution – First Steps

You've taken the first steps, and now you know much more about how codependence forms and how the patterns in your life shaped it. It's extremely important to take a moment to congratulate yourself for the difficult work you've done. Celebrate how you've recognized that your needs *do* matter. That's what drew you to this book and the work we're doing here. You are a brave soul, and you're not alone. There are many people struggling with the same kinds of difficulties you've been experiencing your whole life. That's an important fact to know because often, the abusers of codependents have led them to believe the problem is with them. They are to blame, and no one else behaves that way; that's what they will tell you, but that's a lie. The people who have tried to make you feel responsible are doing so because they have an agenda. They are manipulators, and they want you to need them. That's sad, but it's natural that you might want to help them. They do have a problem, but it's not your job to fix it. I know I was all about helping my mother. It was so important to me to save her from the difficult life we were enduring. If you love someone, that's naturally what you want to do. But it wasn't my job, and it's not your job either.

- You have a right to have your needs met.
- You have a right to have your desires fulfilled.
- You have a right to focus on your own needs.
- You have a right to prioritize your own desires.
- You have a right to make your own choices.
- You have a right to respect and kindness.
- You have a right to love and be loved.
- You have a right to live YOUR life.
- You have a right to be independent.
- You have a right to be free of destructive criticism.
- You have a right to respect.
- You have a right to have other people consider your needs too, even as they focus on their own.
- You have a right to be free of toxic people.
- You have a right to know that you are valuable.
- You have a right to self-compassion.
- You have a right to self-love.
- You have a right to self-forgiveness.
- You have a right to self-worth.
- You have a right to a happy life.

These statements represent your new Bill of Rights. Feel free to add as many as are relevant to your life. This is your commitment to move forward with your personal growth. This is your recognition that you are a valuable, unique, beautiful, and loving soul whose contributions are important and make a difference. This is your declaration of your intention to heal.

From this point, the next steps involve moving forward in the healing process. You've recognized the problem and are committed to solving it. Now, you're turning your attention to the healing work that will repair the damage done by years of emotional and possibly physical abuse. In my next book, *Healing Codependency: How to Resolve Your Childhood Trauma so You Can Start Living Your Best Life,* I will guide you step-by-step through proven techniques for healing your codependency. These are the techniques that worked for me, so I know they can help you, too. Together, we can step into the happier, healthier life that is waiting for us. You can heal, and you can become a strong, independent, and happy person. In this book, I'll take show you:

- How to determine the people and situations who contributed to your codependency.
- How to identify the wounds they created and the emotional triggers that resulted.
- How to defuse those triggers as you embrace your shadow self and rebirth your inner child.
- How to save yourself as you resolve any old, toxic relationships that have been holding you down.
- How to build new, healthy habits to preserve your newfound independence.
- How to keep it real as you face new challenges in life.

You have what you need inside of yourself to heal. All you need now is someone to show you the way. You've already come so far, and there's no turning back now. Welcome to your new life that's just waiting for you to live it. Today is the day you start prioritizing yourself. It is my honor to be by your side as you go through the process. Please feel free to reach out with any comments or questions you have. Here is my Facebook page www.facebook.com/elena.miro.psy. I would also love to hear from you regarding your progress.

I am so honored that you chose my book and trusted me with your time. This is the most valuable thing any of us has, and it is my most sincere intention to make sure you feel your time has been well-spent reading this book. Sometimes, personal growth seems like an invisible process, but if you stick to it, you will wake up one day and find that you are living a happier, healthier life in line with your integrity and dreams. This happened in my life, and I know it will happen for you too. Remember, you are not alone on this journey of healing. Many people walk alongside you, including me. We help each other, and toward that end, it will also help me tremendously if you could leave a review or rating. I know you may be busy, but it will not only help me; it will let other people know that you found the content valuable.

Thank you.

Kind regards,

Elena Miro

References Cited

A Brief Overview of Adult Attachment Theory and Research | R. Chris Fraley. (n.d.).

http://labs.psychology.illinois.edu/~rcfraley/attachment.htm

Bortolon, C. B., Signor, L., De Campos Moreira, T., Figueiró, L. R., Benchaya, M. C., Machado, C. A., Ferigolo, M., & Barros, H. M. T. (2016). Family functioning and health issues associated with codependency in families of drug users. Ciência E Saúde Coletiva, 21(1), 101–107

https://doi.org/10.1590/1413-81232015211.20662014.

Coffman, E., & Swank, J. (2021). Attachment Styles and the Family Systems of Individuals Affected by Substance Abuse. The Family Journal, 29(1), 102–108. https://doi.org/10.1177/1066480720934487.

Dependent Personality Disorder DSM-5 301.6 (F60.7) - Therapedia. (n.d.).

https://www.theravive.com/therapedia/dependent-personality-disorder-dsm--5-301.6-(f60.7).

Family Life Matters: Combating Codependency. (n.d.). www.army.mil. https://www.army.mil/article/137572/family_life_matters_combating_codependency#:~:text=Children%20who%20are%20raised%20to,American%20population%20demonstrates%20codependent%20behavior.

Gordon RM, Spektor V, Luu L (2019) Personality Organization Traits and Expected Countertransference and Treatment Interventions. Int J Psychol Psychoanal 5:039. doi.org/10.23937/2572-4037.1510039.

Knapek E, Kuritárné Szabó I. A kodependencia fogalma, tünetei és a kialakulásában szerepet játszó tényezők [The concept, the symptoms and the etiological factors of codependency]. Psychiatr Hung. 2014;29(1):56-64. Hungarian. PMID: 24670293.

Main, M., & Solomon, J. (1986). Discovery of an insecure-disorganized/disoriented attachment pattern. In T. B. Brazelton & M. W. Yogman (Eds.), *Affective development in infancy* (pp. 95–124). Ablex Publishing.

Mcleod, S., PhD. (2023). Erik Erikson's 8 Stages of Psychosocial Development. Simply Psychology. https://www.simplypsychology.org/erik-erikson.html.

Mikulincer M, Shaver PR. An attachment perspective on psychopathology. *World Psychiatry*. 2012 Feb;11(1):11-5.

doi: 10.1016/j.wpsyc.2012.01.003. PMID: 22294997; PMCID: PMC3266769.

Salomonsson, B. (2018). Psychodynamic Interventions in Pregnancy and Infancy: Clinical and Theoretical Perspectives. Routledge.

https://www.taylorfrancis.com/chapters/mono/10.4324/9781351117142-4/delivery-trauma-maternal-introject-bj%C3%B6rn-salomonsson.

Sjöblom M, Öhrling K, Prellwitz M, Kostenius C. Health throughout the lifespan: The phenomenon of the inner child reflected in events during childhood experienced by older persons. Int J Qual Stud Health Well-being. 2016 Jun 16;11:31486. doi: 10.3402/qhw.v11.31486. PMID: 27317381; PMCID: PMC4912602.

Subramanian, S., & Dewaram Francis Raj, I. (2012). The efficacy of an intervention on healing the inner child on emotional intelligence, and adjustment among the college students. Indian Journal of Health and Wellbeing, 3(3), 648–652.

https://ischolar.in/index.php/ijhw/article/viewFile/49460/40464.

Tonik Web Studio. (n.d.). Lise Bourbeau. Lise Bourbeau. https://www.lisebourbeau.com/en/.

www.ingramcontent.com/pod-product-compliance
Lightning Source LLC
LaVergne TN
LVHW012023060526
838201LV00061B/4437